A-Z WOLVERH

CW00742642

CONTENT

REFERENCE

Motorway	**M6**
A Road	**A41**
B Road	**B4156**
Dual Carriageway	
One Way Street Traffic Flow on A Roads is also indicated by a heavy line on the driver's left.	⇒
Restricted Access	
Pedestrianized Road	
Track or Footpath	
Railway	Level Crossing / Station / Tunnel
Midland Metro The boarding of Metro trams at stops may be limited to a single direction, indicated by the arrow	Stop
Built Up Area	BERRY ST
Local Authority Boundary	—·—·—·—
Posttown Boundary	
Postcode Boundary *within Posttown*	
Map Continuation	**10** Large Scale City Centre **26**

Car Park (Selected)	**P**
Church or Chapel	†
Cycleway (Selected)	⤶⚲
Fire Station	■
Hospital	**H**
House Numbers A & B Roads only	4 36
Information Centre	**i**
National Grid Reference	³90
Park & Ride	Science Park **P+**▭▭▭
Police Station	▲
Post Office	★
Toilet with facilities for the Disabled	▽ ▽
Educational Establishment	▢
Hospital or Hospice	▢
Industrial Building	▥
Leisure or Recreational Facility	▢
Place of Interest	▢
Public Building	▢
Shopping Centre or Market	▢
Other Selected Buildings	▢

SCALE

Map Pages 2-25	Map Page 26
1:15,840 4 inches (10.16 cm) to 1 mile	1:7,920 8 inches (20.32 cm) to 1 mile
0 ¼ ½ Mile	0 ⅛ ¼ Mile
0 250 500 750 Metres	0 100 200 300 Metres
6.31 cm to 1 km	12.63 cm to 1 km

Copyright of Geographers' A-Z Map Company Limited

Head Office:
Fairfield Road, Borough Green, Sevenoaks, Kent TN15 8PP
Telephone: 01732 781000 (Enquiries & Trade Sales)
01732 783422 (Retail Sales)
www.a-zmaps.co.uk
Copyright © Geographers' A-Z Map Co. Ltd. 2004   Edition 1 2004

OS Ordnance Survey® This product includes mapping data licensed from Ordnance Survey® with the permission of the Controller of Her Majesty's Stationery Office.
© Crown Copyright 2004. All rights reserved.
Licence number 100017302

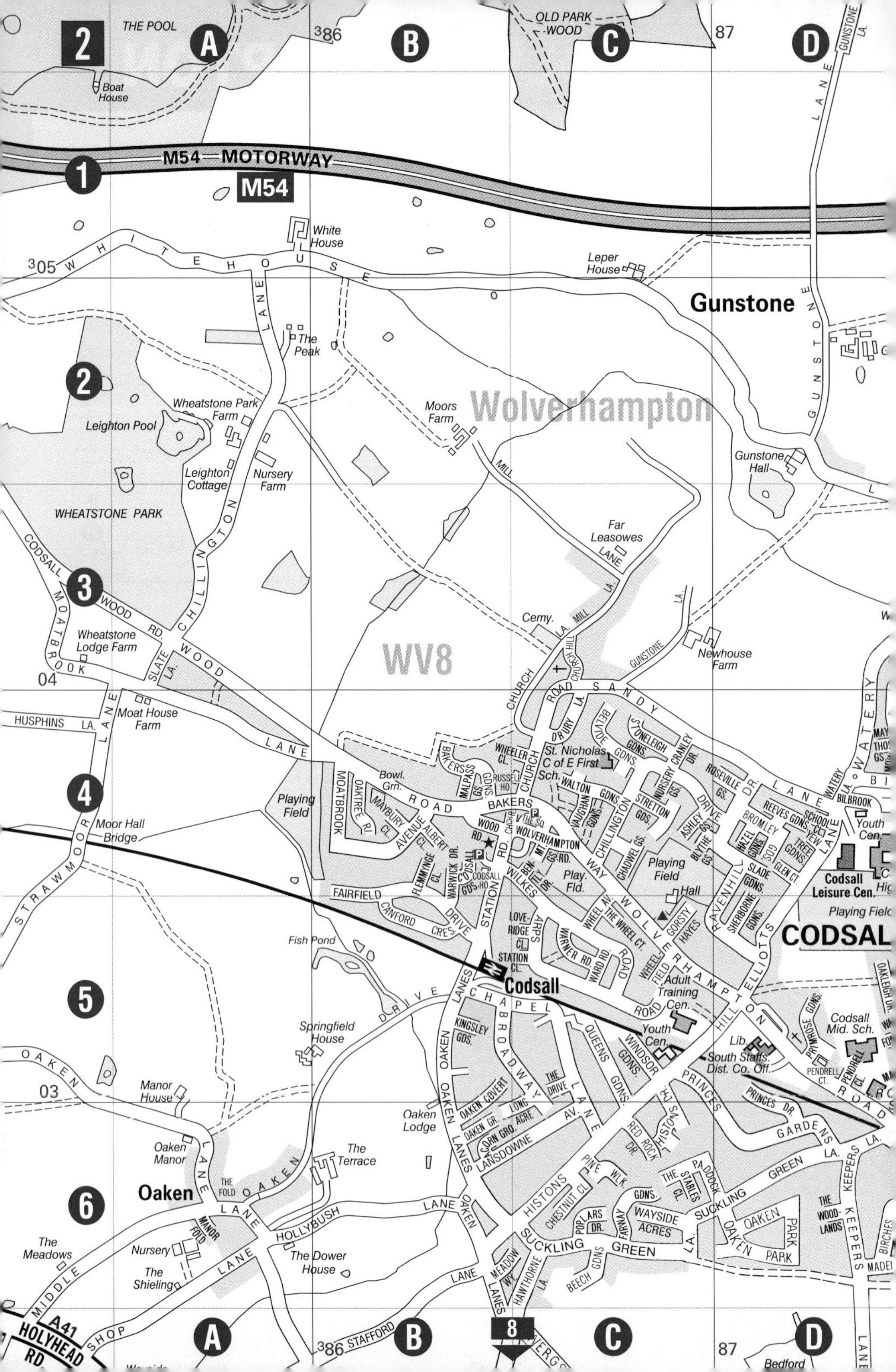
THE POOL
Boat House
386
87
OLD PARK WOOD
M54 MOTORWAY
M54
WHITEHOUSE LANE
White House
305
Leper House
Gunstone
GUNSTONE LANE
The Peak
Wheatstone Park Farm
Leighton Pool
Leighton Cottage
Nursery Farm
WHEATSTONE PARK
Moors Farm
Wolverhampton
MILL LANE
Gunstone Hall
Far Leasowes
CHILLINGTON LANE
CODSALL WOOD RD.
MOATBROOK LANE
Wheatstone Lodge Farm
SLATE LA.
04
Cemy.
WV8
GUNSTONE LA.
Newhouse Farm
HUSPHINS LA.
Moat House Farm
CHURCH ROAD
SANDY LANE
St. Nicholas C of E First Sch.
Bowl. Grn.
Playing Field
BAKERS WAY
WOLVERHAMPTON ROAD
Moor Hall Bridge
STRAWMOOR LANE
FAIRFIELD DRIVE
CANFORD CRES.
STATION RD.
Play. Fld.
Hall
Codsall Leisure Cen.
Youth Cen.
CODSALL
WATERY LANE
BILBROOK
Fish Pond
Codsall
Adult Training Cen.
Springfield House
CHAPEL LANE
BROADWAY
Youth Cen.
Lib.
South Staffs. Dist. Co. Off.
Codsall Mid. Sch.
PRINCES GARDENS
OAKEN LANES
OAKEN LANE
03
Manor House
Oaken Manor
Oaken Lodge
The Terrace
Oaken
HOLLYBUSH LANE
LANSDOWNE AV.
HISTONS HILL
SUCKLING GREEN LA.
WAYSIDE ACRES
OAKEN PARK
THE WOODLANDS
KEEPERS LANE
The Meadows
Nursery
The Shieling
The Dower House
MIDDLE LANE
A41 HOLYHEAD RD
SHOP LANE
STAFFORD LANE
8
Bedford

E
F
G
H
3
88
89
Shropshire Union Canal
The Old Hattons
The Middle Hattons
Lower Hattons Bridge
M54
M54 MOTORWAY
Ring Hill Covert
Farm
Ash Coppice
The Hattons
River Penk
PORT LANE
The Moniepits
PENDEFORD HALL LANE
Island Pool
Upper Hattons Bridge
The Long Wood
The Round Wood
Fish Pond
WV9
04
COVEN LANE
PENDEFORD HALL MOBILE HOME PARK
Moat Brook
Bilbrook
Sewage Works
Playing Field
Pendeford Mill
Pendeford Bridge
WOBASTON ROAD
MILL LANE
JOEY'S LA.
HOMEFIELD RD.
MILL GRO.
Lane Grn. First Sch.
Bilbrook C of E Middle Sch.
LIME TREE GDNS
PENDEFORD LANE
BALLIOL BUSINESS PARK
Depot
Works
Upper Pendeford Farm
Lane Green
FLORENCE RD.
ALEXANDER RD
CLIFTON GDS.
DOWNIE RD.
BROOKFIELD RD
BARNHURST LANE
03
Pendeford
DROVEWAY
Bilbrook
WESLEY ROAD
LANE GREEN ROAD
OAKFIELD AV.
SOUTH VIEW CL.
Filter Tank No. 3
Filter Tank
Turnover Bridge
Weir
THE RYEFIELD
SMALLWOOD RD
MIDDLEFIELD
CORNFIELD
Bilbrook Bridge
9
Sports
1
2
3
4
5
6

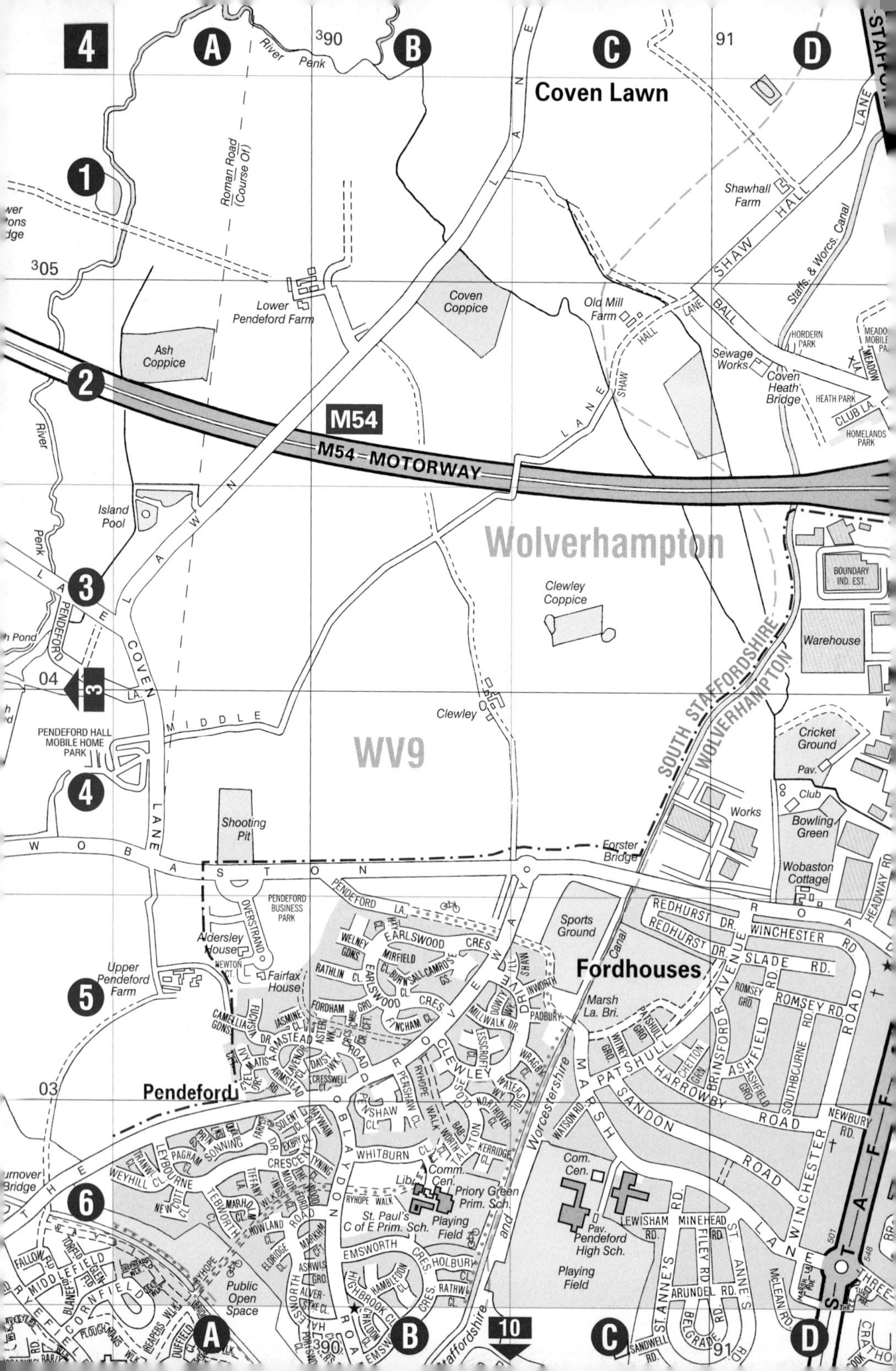

Coven Lawn
River Penk
Roman Road (Course Of)
Lower Pendeford Farm
Ash Coppice
Coven Coppice
M54
M54 MOTORWAY
Shawhall Farm
SHAW HALL LANE
Staffs. & Worcs. Canal
Old Mill Farm
Sewage Works
Coven Heath Bridge
HORDERN PARK
HEATH PARK
CLUB LA.
HOMELANDS PARK
Island Pool
Wolverhampton
Clewley Coppice
BOUNDARY IND. EST.
Warehouse
PENDEFORD LA.
COVEN LANE
MIDDLE LA.
Clewley
PENDEFORD HALL MOBILE HOME PARK
WV9
SOUTH STAFFORDSHIRE
WOLVERHAMPTON
Cricket Ground
Pav.
Club
Bowling Green
Works
Shooting Pit
Forster Bridge
WOBASTON ROAD
Wobaston Cottage
PENDEFORD BUSINESS PARK
OVERSTRAND
Aldersley House
Fairfax House
Upper Pendeford Farm
Sports Ground
Fordhouses
Canal
REDHURST DR.
WINCHESTER RD.
SLADE RD.
ROMSEY RD.
EARLSWOOD CRES.
MIRFIELD CL.
RATHLIN CL.
Marsh La. Bri.
ASHFIELD
SOUTHBOURNE RD.
HARROWBY ROAD
PATSHULL
SANDON ROAD
Pendeford
CLEWLEY DRIVE
PENSHAW CL.
WHITBURN CL.
Comm. Cen.
Priory Green Prim. Sch.
St. Paul's C of E Prim. Sch.
Playing Field
Com. Cen.
Pendeford High Sch.
LEWISHAM RD.
MINEHEAD RD.
ARUNDEL RD.
ST. ANNE'S RD.
MARSH LANE
Worcestershire
Staffordshire and
Public Open Space
EMSWORTH CRES.
HOLBURY CL.
Turnover Bridge
THE WAY
CORNFIELD
BLAYDON ROAD
MIDDLEFIELD
LEYBOURNE CRES.

3
10

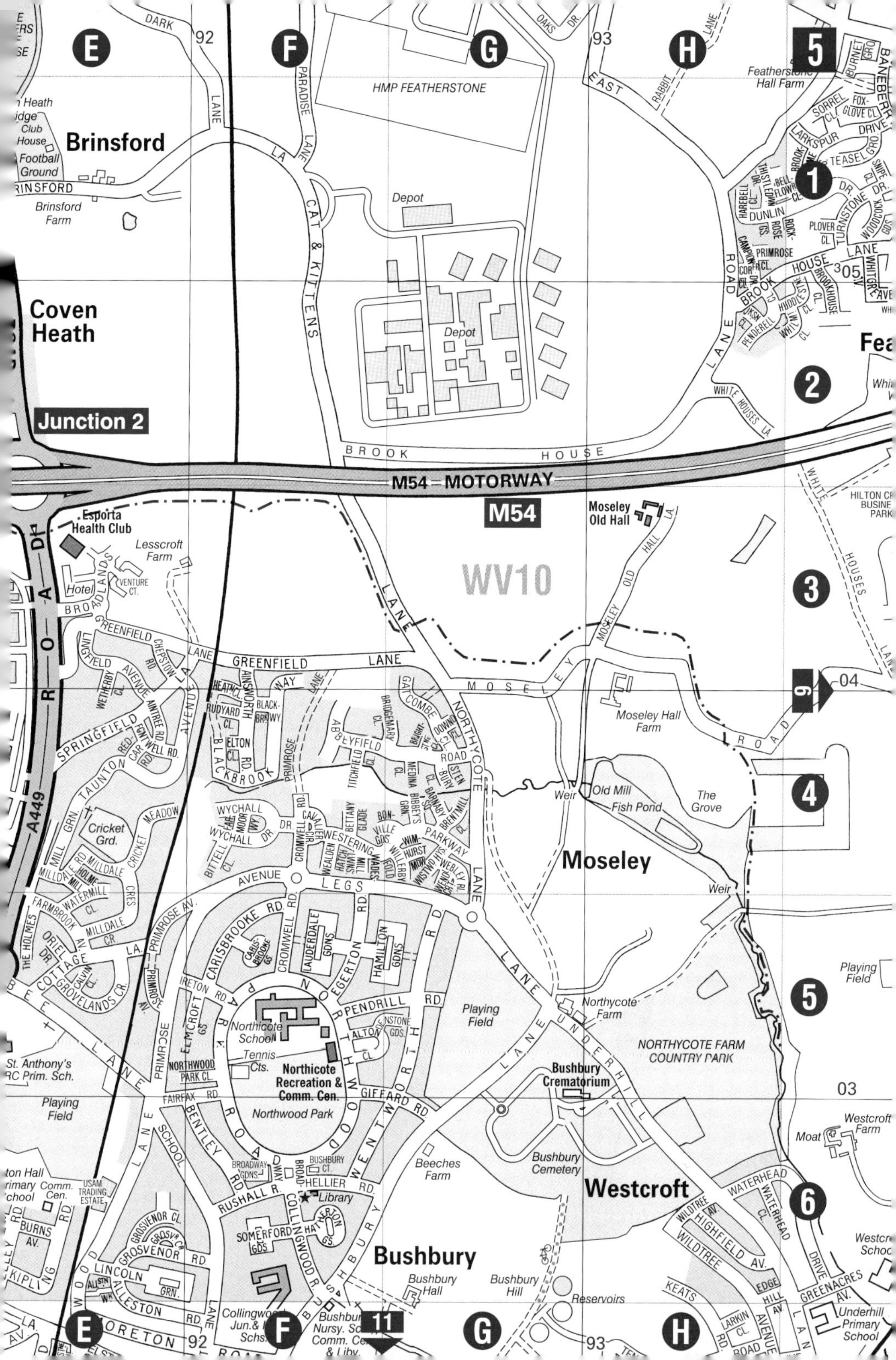

E
F
G
H
5
92
93
Brinsford
Coven Heath
Junction 2
HMP FEATHERSTONE
Depot
Featherstone Hall Farm
Brinsford Farm
Football Ground
M54 MOTORWAY
M54
Esporta Health Club
Lesscroft Farm
Hotel
Moseley Old Hall
WV10
Moseley Hall Farm
Old Mill Fish Pond
The Grove
Weir
Moseley
Cricket Grd.
Northicote School
Tennis Cts.
Northicote Recreation & Comm. Cen.
Northwood Park
Playing Field
Northycote Farm
NORTHYCOTE FARM COUNTRY PARK
Bushbury Crematorium
Bushbury Cemetery
Westcroft
Westcroft Farm
Moat
Beeches Farm
Library
Bushbury
Bushbury Hall
Bushbury Hill
Reservoirs
St. Anthony's RC Prim. Sch.
USAM TRADING ESTATE
Underhill Primary School
A449
BROOK HOUSE
GREENFIELD LANE
MOSELEY ROAD
CAT & KITTENS LANE
NORTHYCOTE LANE
UNDERHILL LANE
LEGS AVENUE
PARK ROAD
NORTHWOOD
WENTWORTH
BUSHBURY
COLLINGWOOD R.
MORETON
03
04
05
1
2
3
4
5
6
9
11

Featherstone Hall Farm
NEW ROAD
94
MONUMENT DR.
SHEPWELL GS.
PARK
395
HILTON PARK
North Lodge
BURNET GRO.
BANEBERRY
SPEEDWELL GS.
PRIMROSE GDS.
DRIVE
HONEYSUCKLE
LIVE & LET LIVE MOBILE HOME PARK
SORREL CL.
FOX-GLOVE CL.
PENNYCRESS GDNS.
CRANESBILL CL.
DAVE
OLD LA.
DARK LANE
The Shrubbery
Lower Lodge
LARKSPUR
DRIVE
TEASEL GRO.
WIDGEON GRO.
Comm. Cen.
THE LEAS
Lower Pool
BROOKLIME GS.
SNIPE CL.
SANDERLING CL.
OLDE HALL RD.
OLDE HALL CT.
CANNOCK ROAD
A460
BELLFLOWER CL.
DUNLIN
HAREBELL CL.
TURNSTONE DRIVE
HILTON
NORTH
ROSE GS.
ROCK-ROSE
PLOVER CL.
WOODCOCK GDS.
OLDE HALL
CRES.
Moat
CAMPION
PRIMROSE CL.
HOUSE LANE
THE AVENUE
305
ROAD
CORF CL.
BROOK
WHITGREAVE AV.
WHITGREAVE AVE
Whitgreave Prim. Sch.
SOUTH CRES.
CRESCENT
SOUTH
Lower Belt
HUDDLESTONE CL.
BROOKHOUSE CL.
WHITGREAVE CT.
SOUTH VW. CL.
Sports Ground
PENDERELL
WHITMORE CL.
Featherstone
HILTON PARK
Old Ride
LANE
WHITE HOUSES LA
Whitgreaves Wood
M54
The Tower
The Rhododendrons
Junction 1
M54 MOTORWAY
WHITE HOUSES LANE
HILTON CROSS BUSINESS PARK
Hill Farm
HILTON CROSS
ROAD
Mill Ride
HILTON MAIN INDUSTRIAL ESTATE
04
5
MOSELEY ROAD
WV10
Fish Pond
BOGNOP
Wolverhampton
The Grove
Mill Farm
Pool Farm
Old Windmill
LANE
Manor Farm
Essington House
Essington Hall Farm
Weir
A460
Playing Field
Sandy Flatts
NORTHYCOTE FARM COUNTRY PARK
03
Moat
HAMPTON
Westcroft Farm
Moat
UNDERHILL
WATERHEAD
WILDTREE AV.
HIGHFIELD AV.
WILDTREE
Westcroft
Westcroft School
WOOD HAYES CFT.
WOOD HAYES
OLD
BLACKHALVE
B41
Blackcove Farm
EDGE HILL
GREENACRES AV.
DRIVE
KEATS
LARKIN CL.
ROAD
AVENUE
Underhill Prim. Sch.
LANE
12
94
395
A
B
C
D
1
2
3
4
5
6

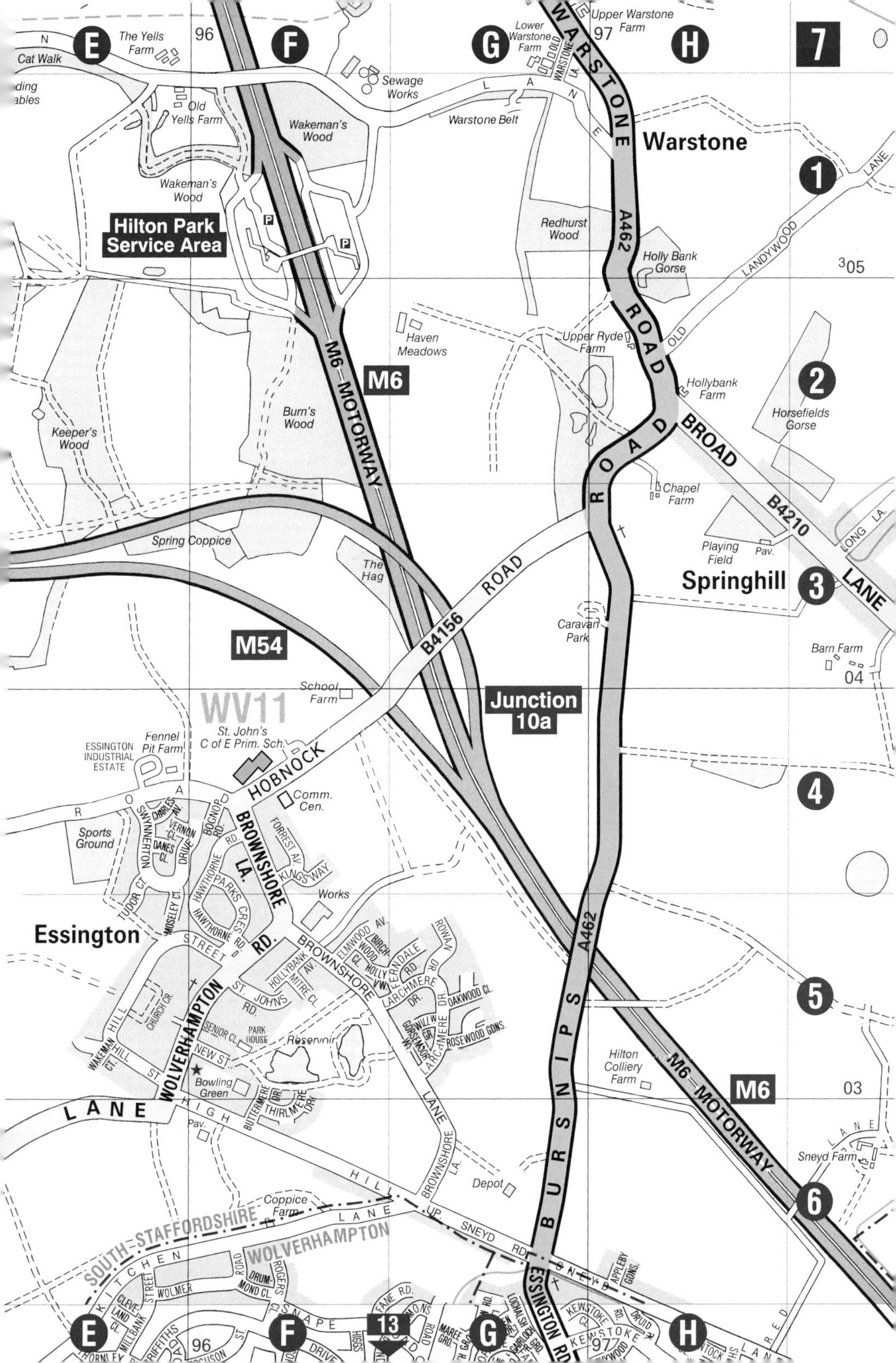

7
E
F
G
H
96
97
1
2
3
4
5
6
The Yells Farm
Cat Walk
Old Yells Farm
Wakeman's Wood
Wakeman's Wood
Hilton Park Service Area
Lower Warstone Farm
Upper Warstone Farm
OLD WARSTONE LA.
Sewage Works
WARSTONE LANE
Warstone Belt
WARSTONE ROAD
Warstone
LANDYWOOD LANE
Redhurst Wood
A462
Holly Bank Gorse
305
Haven Meadows
Upper Ryde Farm
OLD ROAD
Hollybank Farm
Horsefields Gorse
BROAD LANE
B4210
M6 MOTORWAY
M6
Burn's Wood
Keeper's Wood
Chapel Farm
LONG LA.
Spring Coppice
The Hag
Playing Field
Pav.
Springhill
M54
B4156 ROAD
Caravan Park
Barn Farm
04
School Farm
WV11
Junction 10a
Fennel Pit Farm
ESSINGTON INDUSTRIAL ESTATE
St. John's C of E Prim. Sch.
HOBNOCK ROAD
Comm. Cen.
Sports Ground
BROWNSHORE LA.
BOGNOR RD.
FORREST AV.
KINGS WAY
SWYNNERTON
CHARLES AV.
VERNON CL.
DANES CL.
DRIVE
HAWTHORNE RD.
PARKS CRES.
Works
TUDOR CT.
MOSELEY CT.
HAWTHORNE RD.
Essington
STREET
BROWNSHORE LANE
ELMWOOD AV.
BIRCH WOOD
HOLLY VW.
FERNDALE RD.
ROWAN DR.
HOLLYBANK AV.
MITRE CL.
LARCHMERE DR.
OAKWOOD CL.
WOLVERHAMPTON RD.
ST. JOHNS RD.
CHURCH CR.
HILL STREET
SENIOR CL.
PARK HOUSE
NEW ST.
Reservoir
ROSEWOOD GDNS.
WAKEMAN CT.
Bowling Green
BUTTERMERE DR.
THIRLMERE DR.
LANE
HIGH HILL
Pav.
Hilton Colliery Farm
03
BURSNIPS ROAD
A462
Depot
BROWNSHORE LA.
Sneyd Farm
LANE
Coppice Farm
SOUTH STAFFORDSHIRE
LANE
WOLVERHAMPTON
UP. SNEYD RD.
SNEYD LANE
APPLEBY GDNS.
ESSINGTON RD.
KITCHEN LANE
STREET
WOLMER
ROAD
DRUMMOND CL.
ROGERS CL.
CLEVELAND CL.
MILLBANK
SNAPE
FANE RD.
13
LOCHALSH GRO.
KEWSTOKE CL.
KEWSTOKE RD.
DRUID

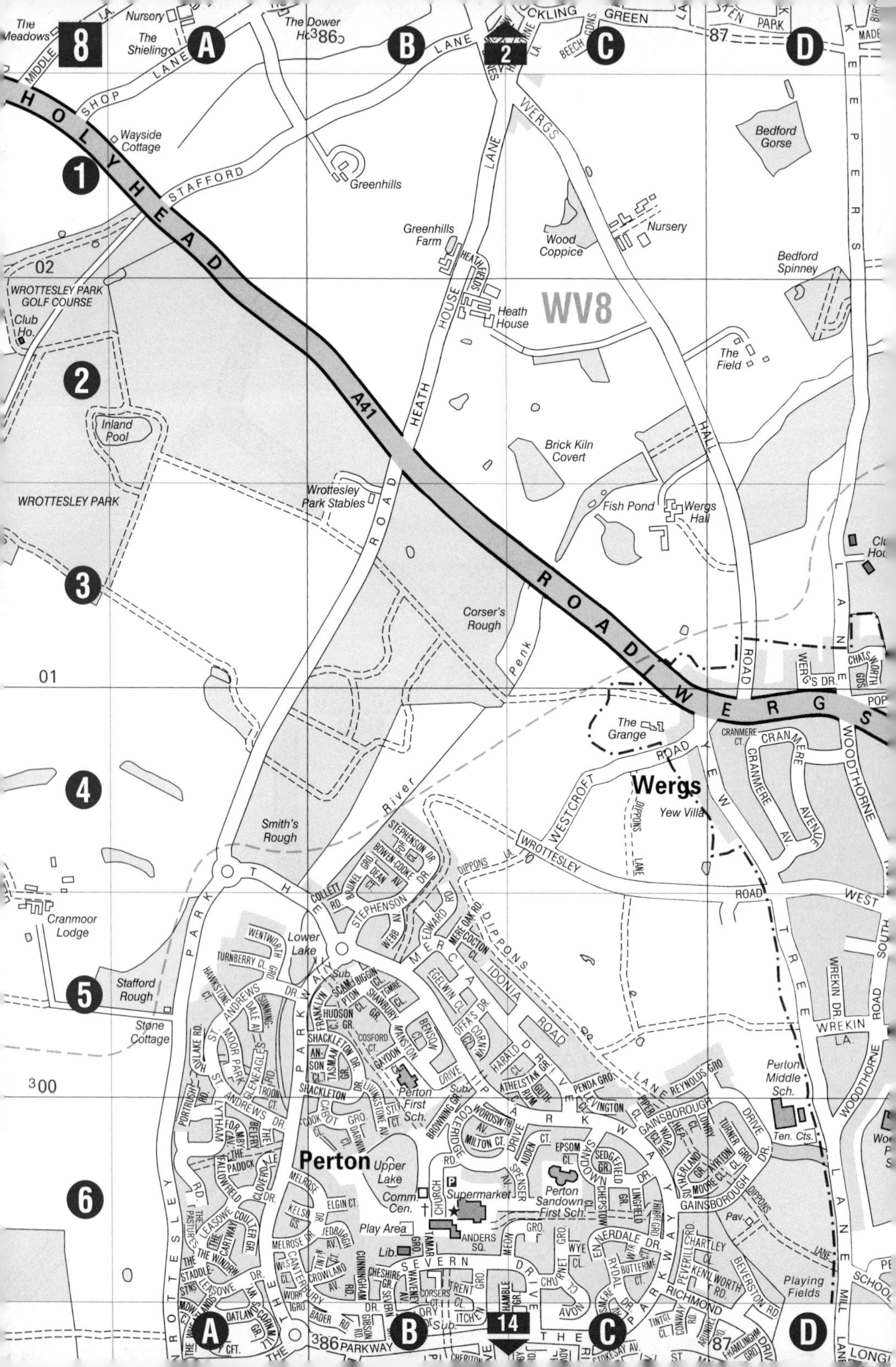

The Meadows
Nursery
The Shieling
The Dower Ho.
386
387
A
B
C
D
2
GREEN
BEECH GDNS.
SHOP LANE
MIDDLE LA.
LANE
Wayside Cottage
Greenhills
HOLYHEAD ROAD
STAFFORD
WERGS LANE
1
Bedford Gorse
Greenhills Farm
Wood Coppice
Nursery
Bedford Spinney
02
WROTTESLEY PARK GOLF COURSE
Club Ho.
HEATHFIELDS
Heath House
WV8
HEATH HOUSE LANE
2
The Field
Inland Pool
A41
Brick Kiln Covert
HALL
WROTTESLEY PARK
Wrottesley Park Stables
Fish Pond
Wergs Hall
ROAD
3
Corser's Rough
Penk
WERGS ROAD
01
WERGS DR.
CHATSWORTH GDS.
The Grange
CRANMERE CT.
CRANMERE AVENUE
CRANMERE AV.
WOODTHORNE
River
WESTCROFT ROAD
Wergs
4
DIPPONS LANE
Yew Villa
YEW TREE
Smith's Rough
WROTTESLEY ROAD
DIPPONS LA.
STEPHENSON DR.
BOWEN-COOKE AV.
BRUNEL GRO.
DEAN CT.
COLLETT RD.
STEPHENSON
WEBB AV.
EDWARD RD.
MERE OAK RD.
COCTON CL.
MERCIA
IDONIA
DIPPONS
WEST
Cranmoor Lodge
Lower Lake
WENTWORTH GRO.
TURNBERRY CL.
PARK
THE PARKWAY
WREKIN DR.
SOUTH ROAD
5
Stafford Rough
HAWKSTONE
ST. ANDREWS DR.
DALE AV.
SUNNINGDALE
FRANKLYN CL.
SCAMPTON
BIGGIN CL.
SHAWBURY GR.
TANGMERE CL.
HUDSON GR.
EGELWIN CL.
OFFA'S DR.
WREKIN LA.
Stone Cottage
HOYLAKE RD.
MOOR PARK
GLENEAGLES
TROON CT.
SHACKLETON DR.
ANSON CL.
TASMAN GR.
COSFORD CT.
GAYDON
MANSTON
BENSON CL.
CORNWALL
HARALD CL.
ATHELSTAN GR.
GUTHRUM
DRIVE
ROAD
PENDA GRO.
LANE
REYNOLDS GRO.
Perton Middle Sch.
300
PORTRUSH RD.
LYTHAM
ST. ANDREWS DR.
BELFRY
FORMBY AV.
SHACKLETON
LIVINGSTONE AV.
Perton First Sch.
BROWNING GR.
COLERIDGE
WORDSWTH AV.
MILTON CT.
KEVINGTON
PIPER CL.
GAINSBOROUGH
LOWRY CL.
TURNER GRO.
CABOT
COOK CT.
DARWIN
Perton
Upper Lake
AUDEN CT.
EPSOM CL.
SEDGEFIELD GR.
SUTHERLAND GR.
AYRTON CL.
MOORE CL.
Ten. Cts.
THE PADDOCK
CLOVERDALE
FALLOWFIELD
6
MELROSE
ELGIN CT.
KELSO GS.
JEDBURGH AV.
Comm. Cen.
CHURCH RD.
Supermarket
SPENSER AV.
Perton Sandown First Sch.
SANDOWN
CHEPSTOW
LINGFIELD
THIRSK GRO.
GAINSBOROUGH
DIPPONS
Pav.
THE PASTURES
THE LEASOWE
COULTER GR.
THE CARTWAY
THE WINDROW
MELROSE DR.
Play Area
TAMAR GRO.
SANDERS SQ.
GRO.
WYE CL.
ENNERDALE DR.
BUTTERMERE CT.
PEVERILL RD.
CHARTLEY CL.
KENILWORTH RD.
BEVERSTON RD.
LANE
SCHOOL
Lib.
SEVERN
MEON DRIVE
STADDLE
LEASOWE DR.
CANTERBURY
CROWLAND AV.
CUNNINGHAM RD.
CHESHIRE GR.
WAVENEY AV.
CORSERS CT.
TRENT CL.
HAMBLE GR.
CHURNET GRO.
RYDAL
RICHMOND
Playing Fields
MILL LANE
OATLANDS
CORMORANT
BADER RD.
GIBSON RD.
SEVERN DR.
ITCHEN
AVON
TINTERN
CONWAY RD.
FRAMLINGHAM
14
THE PARKWAY
Sub.
CFT.
STOKESAY AV.
LONG
WROTTESLEY

Wolverhampton
WV6
Palmer's Cross
Stockwell End
Tettenhall
Newbridge
Birches First Sch.
Dam Mill
The Dingle
River Penk
Black Coppice
Brookside Farm
Palmers Cross Prim. Sch.
Sports Centre
Aldersley High School
Dovecotes Prim. Sch.
Works
WERGS GOLF COURSE
SOUTH STAFFORDSHIRE GOLF COURSE
SOUTH STAFFORDSHIRE
WOLVERHAMPTON
Danescourt Cemetery
Danescourt
Club House
Wolverhampton Cricket Ground
Sports Ground
Claregate Playing Field
St. Joseph's Convent Sch.
Smestow Valley Local Nature Reserve
Wildside Activity Centre
The Giffard RC Primary Sch.
Newbridge Playing Fields
St. Michael's C of E Primary School
Upper Green
Lower Green
The King's C of E School
Running Track
Water Works
Tettenhall College
Playing Field
Christ Church C of E Jun. Sch.
THE WOLVERHAMPTON NUFFIELD HOSPITAL
Tennis & Squash Club
Newbridge Preparatory Sch.
A41
B4161
CODSALL ROAD
PENDEFORD AVENUE
ALDERSLEY AV
TETTENHALL ROAD
THE ROCK

10
A
B
C
D
1
2
3
4
5
6
4
9
16
Oxley
OXLEY PARK GOLF COURSE
DUNSTALL PARK
WOLVERHAMPTON RACE COURSE
Whitmore Reans
Dunstall Hill
WV6
WV1
WV9
WV8
Public Open Space
Playing Field
Pendeford High Sch.
Rake Gate Prim. Sch.
Nursery
Lib.
Dovecotes Prim. Sch.
Day Cen.
SEWAGE WORKS
Tanks
Wharf
Works
Autherley Junc.
Shropshire Union Canal
Oxley Moor Bridge
OXLEY COURT CARAVAN PARK
Aldersley Recreation Centre
Aldersley Bridge
Club.
Valley Park
All Weather Pitches
Games Court
Rifle Range
Aldersley Leisure Village
Aldersley Stadium
Claregate Prim. Sch.
Playing Field
St. Joseph's Convent Sch.
Smestow Valley Local Nature Reserve
Dunstall Water Bridge
Worcestershire Canal
Staffordshire & Worcestershire Canal
Birmingham Canal
Trotting Track
Viaduct
Grandstand
Parade Ring
Wildside Activity Centre
Wulfrun College
RACECOURSE RD. INDUSTRIAL ESTATE
Sports Arena
Wulfruna's Well
DUNSTALL HILL TRADING EST.
The Giffard RC Primary Sch.
Newbridge Playing Fields
St. Michael's C of E Primary School
St. Andrew's C of E Prim. Sch.
Farndale Jun. Sch.
Playground
Warehouse
Dunstall Hill Prim. Sch.
Comm. Cen.
Inf. Sch.
St. Jude's C of E Inf. Sch.
Club House
Oxley Prim. Sch.
Bowling Green
Science Park
WOLVERHAMPTON SCIENCE PARK
Pav.
Ten. Cts.
Lowlands Ct.
Mos.
Lib.
Superstore
FIVE WAYS
STAFFORD ROAD
A449
TETTENHALL ROAD
A41
OXLEY MOOR ROAD
PROBERT ROAD
RENTON ROAD
BLAYDON ROAD
ALDERSLEY ROAD
ALDERSLEY AVENUE
CROSSLAND AVENUE
CROSSLAND CRES.
GREEN LANE
BLACKBURN AVENUE
LAWNSWOOD AV.
BLAKELEY AV.
ST. ANNE'S RD.
RYEFIELD
EASTNEY CRES.
PENDEFORD CL.
MACROME ROAD
EMSWORTH CRES.
HIGHBROOK CL.
ARUNDEL RD.
BELGRADE RD.
SANDWELL RD.
INGESTRE RD.
BARRINGTON CL.
CHURCH GDS.
BEECH RD.
CHURCHFIELD RD.
ECCLESHALL AV.
LODGE RD.
CAPSTONE AV.
BURNHAM AV.
MANOR RD.
GREENWOOD RD.
GREEN DRIVE
RIBBESFORD AV.
DOUGLAS PL.
OXLEY AV.
JONES RD.
SOUTH ST.
COXWELL AV.
DUNSTALL ROAD
GORSEBROOK ROAD
CARTER ROAD
HORDERN ROAD
FARNDALE AVENUE
NEWHAMPTON ROAD WEST
NEW HAMPTON ROAD
SWEETMAN ST.
ALLEN ROAD
NEWBRIDGE CRESCENT
LEICESTER STREET
DUNSTALL STREET
DUNSTALL AVENUE
DUNSTALL HILL
WATERLOO RD.
STAVELEY ROAD
CRADDOCK ST.
GATIS ST.
COLEMAN ST.
COURT RD.
GIBBONS RD.
CROWTHER ROAD
SANDY LA.
LOWLANDS AV.
BURLAND AVENUE
FIVE WAYS

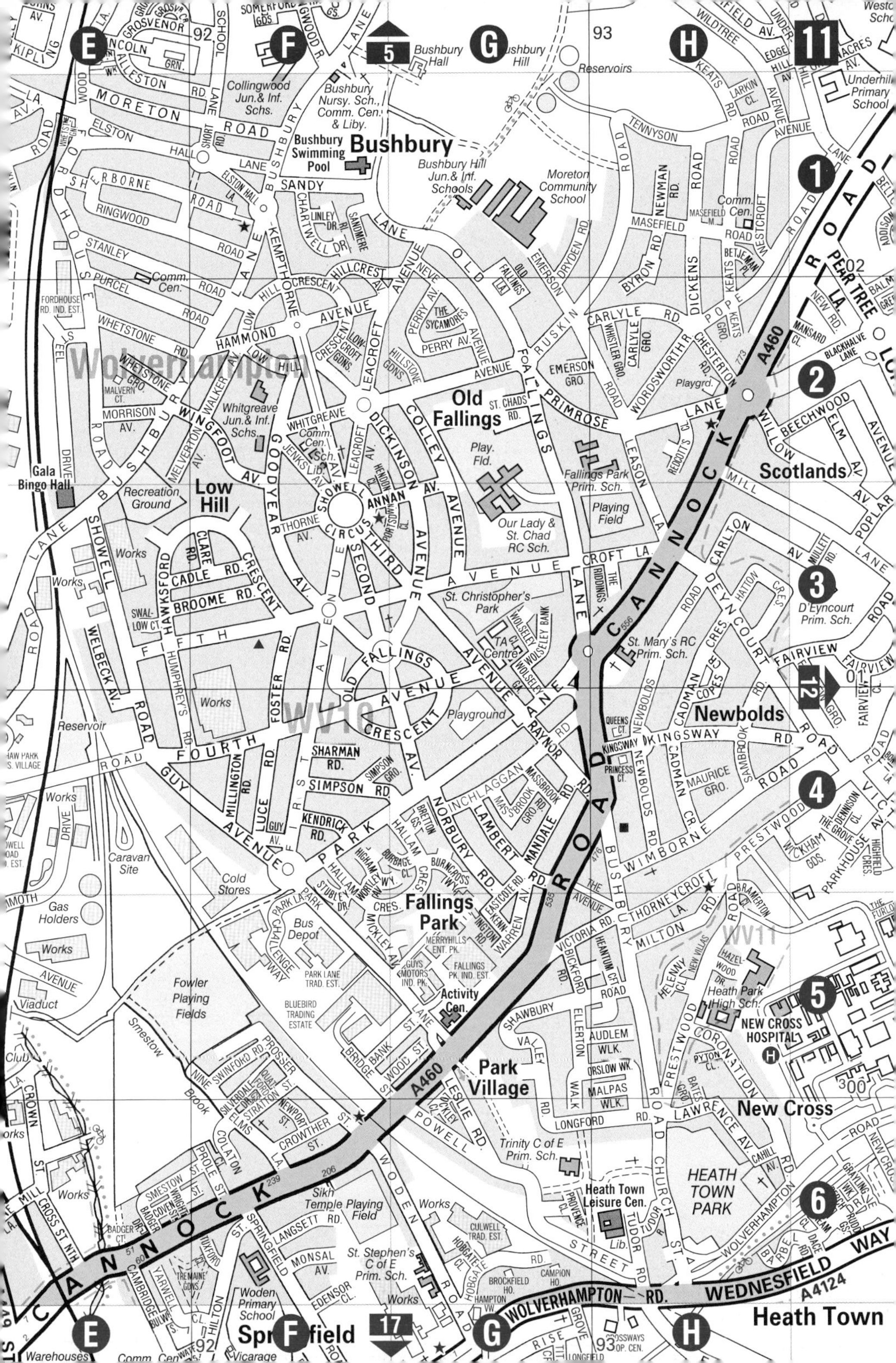

11
5
12
17
E
F
G
H
1
2
3
4
5
6
92
93
Bushbury
Bushbury Hall
Bushbury Hill
Reservoirs
Collingwood Jun.& Inf. Schs.
Bushbury Nursy. Sch., Comm. Cen. & Liby.
Bushbury Swimming Pool
Bushbury Hill Jun.& Inf. Schools
Moreton Community School
Underhill Primary School
Wolverhampton
Old Fallings
Low Hill
Scotlands
Newbolds
Fallings Park
Park Village
New Cross
Heath Town
Springfield
WV10
WV11
Whitgreave Jun.& Inf. Schs.
Comm. Cen.
Gala Bingo Hall
Recreation Ground
Play. Fld.
Fallings Park Prim. Sch.
Playing Field
Our Lady & St. Chad RC Sch.
St. Christopher's Park
TA Centre
St. Mary's RC Prim. Sch.
D'Eyncourt Prim. Sch.
Playground
Playgrd.
Works
Reservoir
Caravan Site
Cold Stores
Gas Holders
Bus Depot
Fowler Playing Fields
Viaduct
Smestow Brook
Park Lane Trad. Est.
Bluebird Trading Estate
Merryhills Ent. Pk.
Fallings Pk. Ind. Est.
Guys Motors Ind. Pk.
Activity Cen.
Fordhouse Rd. Ind. Est.
Heath Park High Sch.
New Cross Hospital
Trinity C of E Prim. Sch.
Heath Town Leisure Cen.
Lib.
Heath Town Park
Sikh Temple Playing Field
St. Stephen's C of E Prim. Sch.
Culwell Trad. Est.
Woden Primary School
Warehouses
Comm. Cen.
Vicarage
Crossways Sh. Cen.
Brockfield Ho.
Campion Ho.
Hampton Vw.
Cannock Road
A460
A4124
Wolverhampton Rd.
Wednesfield Way
Bushbury Lane
Moreton Road
Sherborne Road
Ringwood Road
Stanley Road
Purcel Road
Whetstone Road
Hammond Avenue
Wingfoot Av.
Showell Circus
Goodyear Av.
Second Avenue
Third Avenue
Fifth Avenue
Fourth Avenue
First Avenue
Old Fallings Crescent
Old Fallings Lane
Fallings Lane
Primrose Lane
Croft La.
Park Lane
Guy Avenue
Colley Avenue
Dickinson Av.
Leacroft Avenue
Kempthorne Avenue
Sandy Lane
Tennyson Road
Masefield Road
Carlyle Rd.
Ruskin Avenue
Wordsworth R.
Chesterton Rd.
Dickens Road
Deyncourt Road
Kingsway
Wimborne Road
Thorneycroft La.
Milton Rd.
Victoria Rd.
Prestwood Road
Coronation Road
Church Road
Longford Rd.
Powell St.
Woden Road
Springfield Rd.
Crowther St.
Mill Lane
Showell Road
Welbeck Av.
Hawksford Crescent
Cadle Rd.
Broome Rd.
Norbury Rd.
Lambert Rd.
Mandale Rd.
Raynor Rd.
Sharman Rd.
Simpson Rd.
Kendrick Rd.
Millington Rd.
Luce Rd.
Foster Rd.
Heantun Cft.
Bickford Road
Shawbury Valley
Ellerton Walk
Audlem Wlk.
Orslow Wk.
Malpas Wlk.
Lawrence Av.
Cahill Av.
Tudor Rd.
Street
Beechwood Av.
Willow Av.
Poplar Lane
Carlton Av.
Fairview Rd.
Pear Tree La.
Mansard Cl.
Blackhalve Lane

A
B
C
D
94
395
6
1
2
3
4
5
6
11
18
Westcroft School
Underhill Primary School
WV10
CANNOCK ROAD
A460
B4156
LANE
Oakley Farm
Club.
Sports Ground
GRASSY LA.
BELTON
ADDISON GRO.
SUNDOUR CRES.
WOOD HAYES ROAD
Wood Hayes
BLACKHALVE
PEAR TREE LA.
BALMAIN CR.
GREENS WY.
NEW RD.
MANSARD CL.
Comm. Cen.
MASEFIELD M.
WESTCROFT ROAD
BETJEMAN PL.
KEATS GRO.
POPE
DICKENS
CHESTERTON RD.
LARKIN CL.
UNDERHILL AV.
GREENACRES AV.
Prestwood Farm
Moat
Wolverhampton
SOUTH STAFFORDSHIRE
WOLVERHAMPTON
LONG KNOWLE LANE
B4484
BEALEYS
WHEELER RD.
GOUGH AV.
ARNHEM CL.
BLACKWOOD
GUEST AV.
BEECH TREE AV.
WOOD END ROAD
Prim. Sch.
MEREDITH RD.
AVENUE
HELMS CL.
LEY RD.
Lib.
BRADBURN RD.
MILLS CL.
RYDAL CL.
GRASMERE CL.
HARPER AV.
THE GARLANDS
LOWER PRESTWOOD RD.
LINTHOUSE
PRESTWOOD AV.
RIDGE LA.
DUCKHOUSE RD.
SPRINGHILL
MERCER GRO.
SUDBURY CL.
SPONDON
SHARDLOW RD.
OVERSEAL
BRAILSFORD
MEASHAM WY.
Devil's Elbow Bridge
WOOTTON AV.
MASON CL.
THOMAS
SHEILA AV.
JANINE AV.
RODERICK DR.
Depot
MOAT GRN. AV.
OLINTHUS
MOAT HOUSE LANE EAST
Moat House Prim. Sch.
Scotlands
BEECHWOOD
ELM AV.
AVENUE
WILLOW AV.
POPLAR AV.
OAK GRO.
MILL
CARLTON AV.
MULLETT RD.
Wood End Prim. School
Wood End
LONG MILL NTH.
LONG MILL AV.
LONG MILL S.
D'Eyncourt Prim. Sch.
DEYNCOURT
AMOS
AMOS AV.
ROBIN GRO.
ORCHARD
HAZEL GR.
CHESTNUT GR.
CHERRY GR.
JAYNE CL.
RIDGE LA.
MOAT HOUSE LANE W.
Sch.
BELLAMY
BELLAMY LA.
CEDAR WY.
EXMOOR GN.
SUFFOLK CL.
Playing Field
Sports Ground
HENFIELD CL.
WOLLASTON CRES.
FAIRVIEW
FAIRVIEW GRO.
FAIRVIEW CL.
FAIRVIEW CR.
Newbolds
KINGSWAY
LAMBROOK
MAURICE GRO.
WIMBORNE
ROAD
Football Ground
Playing Field
Woden Ho.
Wodensfield Prim. Sch.
WODEN CRES.
COTTAGE CL.
EVERSLEY GRO.
WODEN WY.
NORTH AV.
EAST AV.
WEST AV.
NORDLEY
MATTOX ROAD
HYLSTONE
HYDE
WRIGHT AV.
DAVENPORT RD.
DAY AV.
DUDLEY GR.
WV11
BROOM HALL AV.
CRES.
PRITCHARD
A4124
LICHFIELD ROAD
THETFORD GDS.
WEM GDS.
LEWIS GRO.
LANE
TITHE RD.
HAMSTEAD CL.
LICHFIELD
B4484
RD.
Wednesfield Park
Wednesfield High School (Upper)
CAROL GR.
HOPTON CR.
BONNY STILE LA.
PRESTWOOD
VICTORIA
VICARAGE
DENNISON
THE GROVE
WICKHAM GDS.
PARKHOUSE AV.
HIGHFIELD CRES.
SCHOOL RD.
LICHFIELD RD.
Wednesfield Village Prim. Sch.
Playing Field
WEDNESFIELD
Wednesfield High School (Lower)
Sports Centre
BRAMERTON
THE FURLONGS
TAYLOR ST.
DUKE ST.
PINFOLD GDS.
HALECROFT AV.
THISTLE CFT.
BLUEBELL CRES.
GREEN MDW.
NORDLEY RD.
FREDERICK RD.
SOUTH AV.
WALK
St. Patrick's RC Prim. School
GRAISELEY ROAD
HAZELWOOD DR.
Heath Pk. High Sch.
NEW CROSS HOSPITAL
MEMORY LA.
Cemy.
FROME DR.
PLYM
BRAY HO.
WILLIAM BENTLEY CT.
CHURCH LANE
HIGH STREET
NEACHELLS
PORTCHESTER DR.
PICKERING RD.
GROSVENOR CT.
GREGORY CT.
March End
LYD CL.
WODENSFIELD TOWER
THRUSHEL WK.
TORRIDGE DR.
NICHOLLS FLD.
Comm. Cen.
WOODHOUSE FOLD
Mkt.
MARCH END RD.
MARCH END RD.
LAKEFIELD
CORONATION
RYTON CL.
NEW HEATH
OKEMENT DR.
Lib.
ALFRED
SQUIRE
HEATHER CL.
COLTS FOOT CL.
FOXGLOVE CL.
YALE
TEAS.
New Cross
300
ROOKERY ST.
BACKHOUSE LA.
Superstore
HALL ST.
WELL LA.
BOLTON ROAD
LAWFRED AV.
WADDENS
LAWRENCE AV.
WV10
WOLVERHAMPTON RD.
NEW CROSS AV.
Cineworld Cinema
Bentley Bri. Leisure Pk.
BENTLEY BRI. WY.
KENMARE WY.
WELL LA.
WEDNESFIELD WAY IND. EST.
HART RD.
SEAMLESS DR.
MERRILL'S HALL LA.
WEDNESFIELD WY.
CAHILL AV.
HEATH TOWN PARK
GRAYLING
PERCH
BREAM
DACE
BARBEL RD.
WEDNESFIELD WAY
A4124
BACKHOUSE LA.
STEELPARK WAY
PLANETARY RD.
PLANETARY
Works
Warehouse
WV13
SATELLITE IND. PARK
NEACHELLS LANE INDUSTRIAL ESTATE
Works
Heath Town
PLANETARY INDUSTRIAL ESTATE
PHOENIX ROAD INDUSTRIAL ESTATE
ROAD
Brook

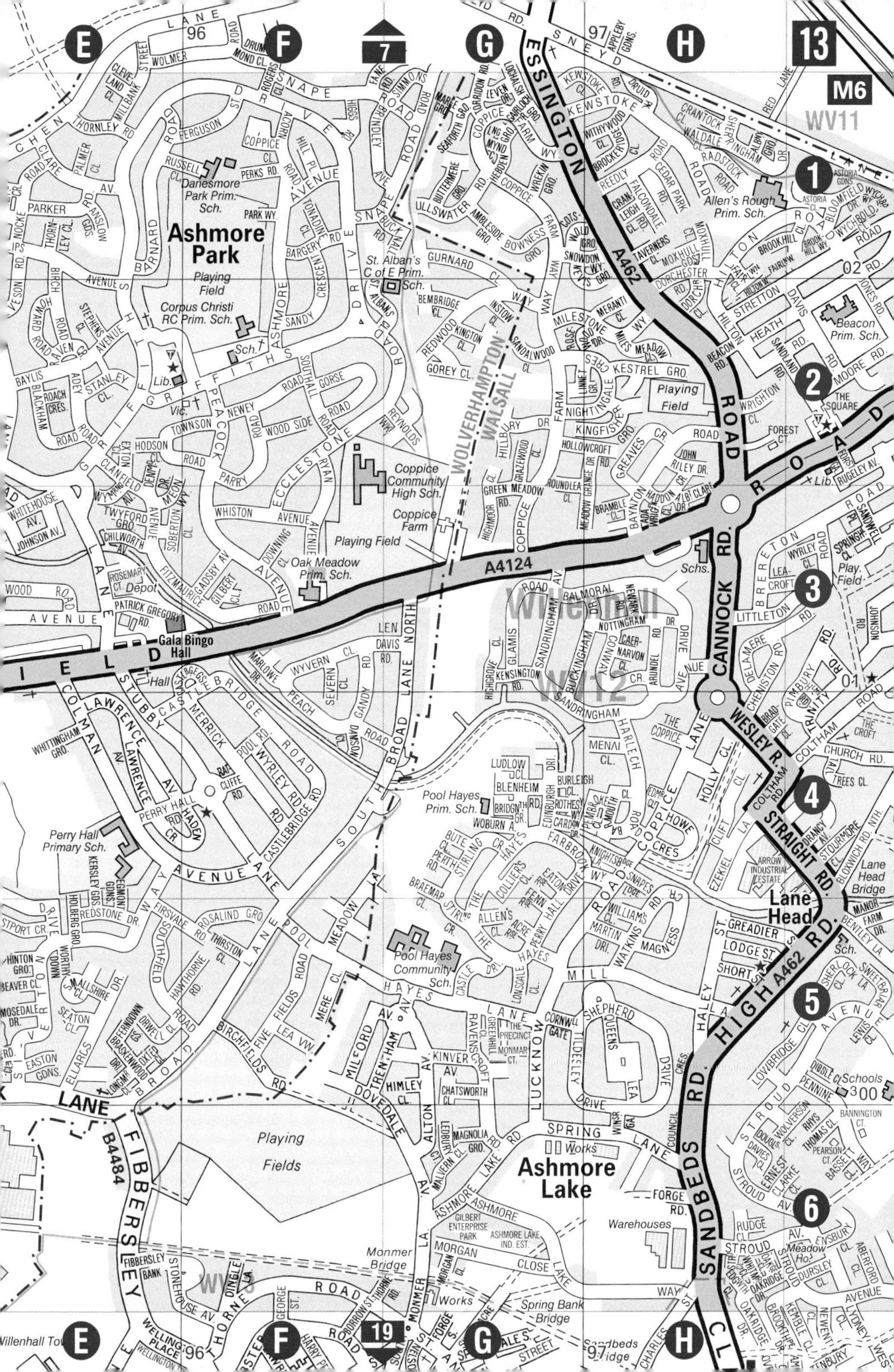
13
E
F
G
H
7
19
96
97
M6
WV11
WV12
1
2
3
4
5
6
Ashmore Park
Ashmore Lake
Lane Head
Willenhall
A462
A4124
B4484
ESSINGTON ROAD
CANNOCK RD.
CANNOCK ROAD
WOLVERHAMPTON
WALSALL
SNEYD LANE
SNAPE ROAD
SNAPE DRIVE
GRIFFITHS DRIVE
ASHMORE AVENUE
ECCLESTONE ROAD
WHISTON AVENUE
PEACOCK ROAD
BARNARD ROAD
SOUTHALL ROAD
GORSE ROAD
WOOD SIDE
NEWEY ROAD
TOWNSON ROAD
PARRY ROAD
HODSON
RYAN AVENUE
DOWNING AVENUE
GADSBY AV.
GILBERT CL.
FITZMAURICE
ROSEMARY CT.
PATRICK GREGORY RD.
Depot
Gala Bingo Hall
Hall
STUBBY LANE
COLMAN AV.
LAWRENCE AV.
WHITTINGHAM GRO.
CASTLEBRIDGE ROAD
CASTLEBRIDGE RD.
MERRICK
WYRLEY RD.
POOL RD.
RATCLIFFE RD.
PERRY HALL RD.
HADEN CR.
Perry Hall Primary Sch.
KERSLEY GDS.
EGMONT GDNS.
REDSTONE DR.
HOLBERG GRO.
ROSALIND GRO.
FIRSVALE RD.
THIRSTON CL.
SOUTHFIELD
HAWTHORNE RD.
ORWELL CL.
MALLSHIRE DR.
BEAVER CL.
MOSEDALE DR.
SEATON CL.
EASTON GDNS.
ELLARLS
FERNDOWN
BRASKENWOOD
LONGMI...
AVENUE LANE
BROAD LANE
BIRCHFIELDS RD.
FIVE FIELDS ROAD
LEA VW.
POOL MEADOW
SOUTH BROAD LANE NORTH
LEN DAVIS RD.
WYVERN CL.
SEVERN CL.
GANDY ROAD
PEACH
MARLOWE DR.
DAWSON CL.
Pool Hayes Prim. Sch.
Pool Hayes Community Sch.
HAYES LANE
MERE CL.
MILFORD AV.
TRENTHAM AV.
HIMLEY CL.
DOVEDALE
ALTON AV.
KINVER AV.
CHATSWORTH CL.
LEDBURY CL.
MAGNOLIA GRO.
MALVERN CL.
RAVENSCROFT
GREENHILL
THE PRECINCT
MONMAR CT.
LUCKNOW ROAD
CORNWALL GATE
SHEPHERD
QUEENS
TILDESLEY DRIVE
SPRING LANE
Works
Playing Fields
FIBBERSLEY
FIBBERSLEY BANK
STONEHOUSE AV.
DINGLE
THORNE LA.
GEORGE ST.
MORGAN CL.
MORGAN CLOSE
Monmer Bridge
GILBERT ENTERPRISE PARK
ASHMORE LAKE IND. EST.
ASHMORE LAKE RD.
Spring Bank Bridge
Warehouses
FORGE RD.
COUNCIL CRES.
SANDBEDS RD.
HIGH RD.
Sandbeds Bridge
CHARLES ST.
WELLINGTON
Willenhall Tow...
STROUD AVENUE
STROUD AV.
ERNEST
CLARKE
RUDGE CL.
DOUGLAS
WOLVERSON CL.
RHYS
THOMAS CL.
PEARSON CT.
BASSETT WAY
BANNINGTON CT.
LOWBRIDGE CL.
PENNINE
Schools
SHERLOCK LA.
SWEETBRIAR
LEWIS CL.
OAKRIDGE DR.
DURSLEY CL.
ABERFORD CL.
LYDNEY AVENUE
NEWENT CL.
KEMBLE CL.
TENBURY
ENSBURY
Meadow Ho.
LODGE ST.
SHORT ST.
GREADIER
HALEY LA.
BENTLEY LA.
MANOR FARM DR.
Lane Head Bridge
BLOXWICH RD. NTH.
STOURMORE
STRAIGHT RD.
ARROW INDUSTRIAL ESTATE
EZEKIEL LA.
CLIFT
COLTHAM RD.
COLTHAM
CHURCH RD.
TALL TREES CL.
THE CROFT
WESLEY R.
TRINITY RD.
PIMBURY RD.
CHENISTON RD.
DELAMERE
LITTLETON
BRERETON ROAD
WYRLEY CL.
LEACROFT
SPRINGHILL CL.
SANDWELL
Play. Field
JOHNSON
SANDRINGHAM AVENUE
SANDRINGHAM
BALMORAL
NEWARK RD.
NOTTINGHAM DR.
BUCKINGHAM
CONWAY
CAERNARVON CR.
ARUNDEL RD.
GLAMIS
KENSINGTON RD.
HIGHGROVE CL.
HARLECH
MENAI CL.
THE COPPICE
HOLLY CL.
LUDLOW CL.
BLENHEIM
BURLEIGH CL.
WOBURN A.
EDINBURGH
COPPICE LANE
HOWE CRES
FARBROOK WY.
KNIGHTSBRIDGE LA.
SNAPES LODGE
WILLIAMS RD.
MARTIN DRI.
WATKINS
MAGNESS CR.
STIRLING CR
BUTE CL.
PERTH RD.
BRAEMAR CL.
COLLIERS CL.
THE ALLEN'S CL.
ACRE RISE
FENN RISE
EATON RISE
PERRY HALL DRIVE
HAYES
CASTLE DR.
LONSDALE CL.
MILL
GREEN MEADOW RD.
HIGHMOOR
HILLBURY DR.
GRAZEWOOD CL.
ROUNDLEA CL.
MEADOW GRANGE DR
HOLLOWCROFT RD.
FARM
NIGHTINGALE
KINGFISHER
GREAVES CR.
JOHN RILEY DR.
BRAMBLE CL.
BAYNTON
HADDON CR.
Playing Field
KESTREL GRO.
LINNET GRO.
MILESTONE WY.
SANDALWOOD
MILES MEADOW
COPPICE FARM WAY
INSTOW
KINGTON CL.
REDWOOD
GOREY CL.
BEMBRIDGE CL.
GURNARD CL.
BOWNESS GRO.
SNOWDON WY.
AMBLESIDE GRO.
ULLSWATER GRO.
BUTTERMERE GRO.
WREKIN GRO.
HEBDEN GRO.
SEAFORTH GRO.
TORRIDON RD.
LEVEN DR.
LOCHALSH GRO.
COPPICE
St. Alban's C of E Prim. Sch.
ST. ALBANS RD.
Coppice Community High Sch.
Coppice Farm
Oak Meadow Prim. Sch.
REYNOLDS
BRINDLEY AVE
FANE RD.
SIMMONS ROAD
HIGGS
ROGERS CL.
DRUMMOND CL.
WOLMER ROAD
MILLBANK STREET
CLEVELAND CL.
THORNLEY RD.
PALMER CL.
CLARE ROAD
PARKER
ANSLOW GDS.
THORNLEY CL.
BIRCH AVENUE
HOWARD ROAD
STEPHENS CL.
RAVEN CL.
ADEY
STANLEY CL.
BAYLIS AVENUE
BLACKHAM ROAD
ROACH CRES.
Lib.
Vic.
EXTON
CLANFIELD AV.
TWYFORD GRO.
CHILWORTH AV.
WHITEHOUSE AV.
JOHNSON AV.
WOOD ROAD
MEON
DENMORE AVENUE
SOBERTON WY.
Danesmore Park Prim. Sch.
RUSSELL CL.
FERGUSON
PERKS RD.
PARK WY.
COPPICE CL.
ACORN
HILL PL.
TONADINE
BARGERY RD.
CRESCENT
SANDY
Corpus Christi RC Prim. Sch.
Sch.
Playing Field
KEWSTOKE RD.
KEWSTOKE CL.
DRUID
WITHYWOOD CL.
BROCKERIDGE
REEDLY
CRANLEIGH CL.
FALCONDALE RD.
CEDAR PARK RD.
TAVERNERS CL.
MOXHULL
DORCHESTER RD.
CRANTOCK
SHERINGHAM
WALDALE
RADSTOCK
ALBANY DR.
Allen's Rough Prim. Sch.
ASTORIA GDNS
BLOOMFIELD
WYCHBOLD
HILTON ROAD
BROOKHILL CL.
FAIRVIEW
STRETTON
HEATH
DAVIS
Beacon Prim. Sch.
BEACON RD.
SANDLAND RD.
MOORE RD.
THE SQUARE
FOREST CT.
WRIGHTON CL.
RUGELEY AV.
APPLEBY GDNS.
RED LANE
Schs.

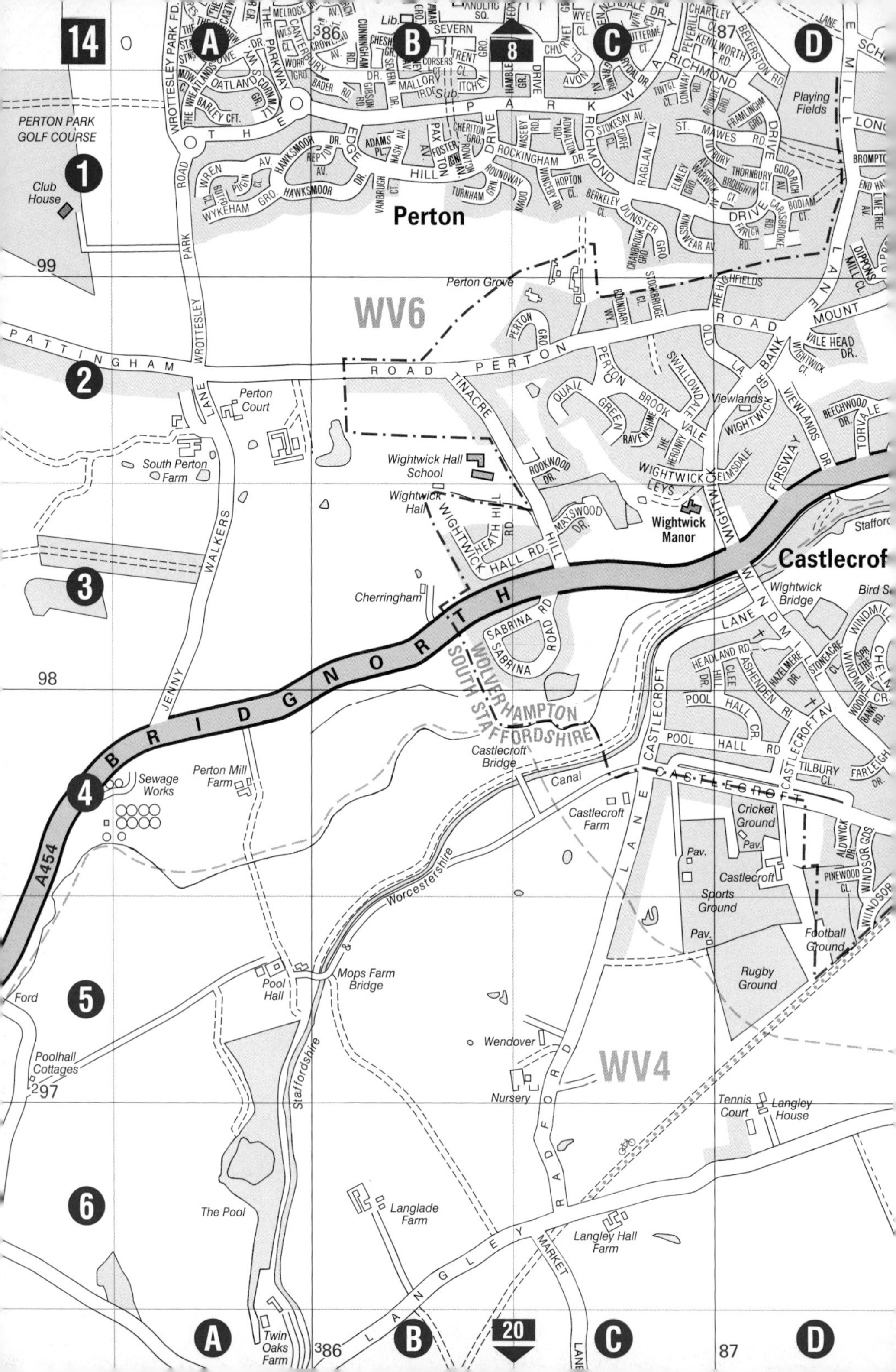

8
20
A
B
C
D
1
2
3
4
5
6
PERTON PARK GOLF COURSE
Club House
Perton
WV6
WV4
Perton Grove
PATTINGHAM ROAD
WROTTESLEY PARK RD.
THE PARKWAY
PARK DRIVE
EDGE HILL DR.
RICHMOND DRIVE
ROCKINGHAM DR.
HAWKSMOOR DR.
WYKEHAM GRO.
Playing Fields
PERTON ROAD
OLD HIGHFIELDS ROAD
MOUNT ROAD
WIGHTWICK BANK
VALE HEAD DR.
Viewlands
VIEWLANDS DR.
FIRSWAY
TORVALE
BEECHWOOD DR.
Perton Court
South Perton Farm
WALKERS LANE
JENNY WALKERS LANE
TINACRE HILL
Wightwick Hall School
Wightwick Hall
WIGHTWICK HALL RD.
HEATH HILL RD.
ROOKWOOD DR.
MAYSWOOD DR.
SWALLOWDALE
QUAIL GREEN
BROOK VALE
RAVENSHIME
THE HERONRY
WIGHTWICK LEYS
ELMSDALE
Wightwick Manor
Castlecroft
Wightwick Bridge
WINDMILL LANE
Cherringham
BRIDGNORTH ROAD
A454
SABRINA ROAD
WOLVERHAMPTON
SOUTH STAFFORDSHIRE
Castlecroft Bridge
Canal
Sewage Works
Perton Mill Farm
Castlecroft Farm
CASTLECROFT LANE
CASTLECROFT RD.
CASTLECROFT AV.
POOL HALL RD
POOL HALL CR.
HEADLAND RD.
ASHENDEN RI.
HAZELMERE DR.
TILBURY CL.
FARLEIGH DR.
Cricket Ground
Pav.
Castlecroft Sports Ground
Football Ground
Rugby Ground
Staffordshire & Worcestershire
Mops Farm Bridge
Pool Hall
Ford
Poolhall Cottages
Wendover
Nursery
RADFORD ROAD
Tennis Court
Langley House
Langlade Farm
The Pool
LANGLEY ROAD
MARKET LANE
Langley Hall Farm
Twin Oaks Farm
99
98
97
86
87

15
9
21
16
E
F
G
H
1
2
3
4
5
6
88
89
97
98
99
Christ Church C of E Jun. Sch.
THE WOLVERHAMPTON NUFFIELD HOSPITAL
Tennis & Squash Club
Newbridge Preparatory Sch.
Newbridge
St. Edmund's Catholic School
St. Peter's Collegiate School
Wolverhampton Girls' High School
Compton Park Rec. Cen.
City of Wolverhampton College (Paget Road Campus)
St. Jude's C of E Jun. Sch.
Tennis Courts
University of Wolverhampton (Compton Park Campus)
City of Wolverhampton College (The Cedars, Horticultural Unit)
Tettenhall Wood School
Tettenhall Wood
The Laurels
Compton
Hospice
Hill House
Graiseley
Leisure and Picnic Area
Valley Park
Smestow
Worcestershire Canal
Wightwick Family Park
Central Park
Nursery
Smestow School
Castlecroft Prim. Sch.
Westacre Inf. Sch.
Uplands Jun. Sch.
Wolverhampton
WV3
BANTOCK PARK
Bantock Ho. Mus
Library
Bradmore
Bhyll's Acre Primary School
Merry Hill
St. Michael's RC Prim. Sch.
Five Ways
Warstones Primary School
Bradmore Rec. Grd.
Windsor Avenue Playing Fields
Warstones Green
Comm. Cen.
Lib.
Highfields School
A454
A41
B4161
COMPTON ROAD
WEST COMPTON ROAD
HENWOOD ROAD
FINCHFIELD HILL
FINCHFIELD ROAD WEST
FINCHFIELD ROAD
BROAD LANE
CASTLECROFT ROAD
UPLANDS AVENUE
COALWAY ROAD
TRYSULL ROAD
WARSTONES DRIVE
WARSTONES ROAD
BIRCHES
CLARK ROAD
PAGET RD.
COMPTON PARK
YORK AVENUE
RICHMOND ROAD
FINCHFIELD LANE
WOODLAND RD.
WOOTTON RD.
ADAMS RD.
WYCHBURY RD.
VICTORIA
OXBARN
ROWAN CRESCENT
HAZEL RD.
WINDSOR AVENUE
LEIGHTON
FIELDS DRIVE
BOUNDARY WAY
SWANCOTE DR.
HIGHGATE AV.
WOLVERLEY AV.

16
A
B
C
D
10
22
15
26
1
2
3
4
5
6
390
391
WV6
WV3
WV4
Park Dale
Merridale
Wolverhampton
Bradmore
BANTOCK PARK
Bantock Ho. Mus.
Library
Blakenhall
Penn Fields
Goldthorn Hill
TETTENHALL ROAD
A41
COMPTON ROAD
A454
CHAPEL ASH
WEST PARK
Fish Ponds
Bandstand
West Park Rehabilitation Hosp.
Eye Inf.
Wolverhampton Wanderers FC (Molineux)
Central Baths
Superstore
Wolverhampton Grammar School
Playing Field
Sports Ground
Sports Grd.
St. Peter's Collegiate School
Wolverhampton Girls' High School
Compton Park Rec. Cen.
City of Wolverhampton College (Paget Road Campus)
St. Jude's C of E Jun. Sch.
Merridale Prim. Sch.
CEMETERY
Mosque
Sikh Temple
Hindu Temple
The Orchard Cen.
Brewery
Royal Wolverhampton Jun. Sch.
The Royal Wolverhampton School
St. Luke's C of E Prim. Sch.
Penn Fields Sch.
Bradmore Rec. Grd.
Memorial Gdns.
Woodfield Jun.& Inf. Schs.
Woodfield Social and Sports Club
Graiseley Rec. Cen.
Blakenhall Rec. Grd.
BIRCHES BARN ROAD
B4161
STUBBS RD.
PENN ROAD
A449
GOLDTHORN HILL
A4039
RING RD. ST. MARKS
RING RD. ST. ANDREWS
COALWAY ROAD
FINCHFIELD ROAD
MERRIDALE ROAD
MERRIDALE STREET
GREAT BRICKKILN STREET
NEW HAMPTON ROAD EAST
PARK ROAD WEST
PARK ROAD EAST
CLARK ROAD

17
E
F
G
H
11
Heath Town
Springfield
WOLVERHAMPTON
Wolverhampton
WV10
WV1
WV2
WEDNESFIELD RD.
CANNOCK ROAD
WOLVERHAMPTON RD.
WEDNESFIELD ROAD
A4124
Woden Primary School
Vicarage
Comm. Cen.
Warehouses
Coach Sta.
Royal Mail Sorting Office
Works
Wyrley & Essington Canal
MANDERS INDUSTRIAL ESTATE
NEW CROSS IND. EST.
CROSSWAYS SHOP. CEN.
ASHBOURNE RD.
BRICKHEATH RD.
BURCOT AV.
ST GILES RD.
DEANSFIELD RD.
EASTFIELD RD.
COLLIERY RD.
STANTON RD.
RING ROAD ST. DAVIDS
RING ROAD ST. PATRICKS
A454
HORSELEY FLDS. LWR. HORSELEY FLD.
WILLENHALL ROAD
A454
ESSINGTON
Play Fld.
Schs.
Corser St.
St. Georges
Super-store
Bus Sta.
Depot
A4150
RING ROAD ST. GEORGES
26
BILSTON ROAD
A41
The Royal
WALSALL STREET
CHILLINGTON WORKS INDUSTRIAL ESTATE
PARKSIDE INDUSTRIAL ESTATE
BI-TEC IND. PK.
CHANCEL IND. EST.
EAST PARK TRADING ESTATE
Holy Rosary RC Prim. Sch.
EAST PARK
Tennis Cts.
Clock Tower
18
Plascom
PARKLANDS
EAST PARK WAY
Warehouse
Monmore Green
Monmore Green Stadium
Wholesale Market
AVENUE
Canal
Birmingham
AMF Bowling
ALL SAINTS' ROAD
All Saints' Prim. Sch.
St. Mary & St. Johns RC Prim. Sch.
Grove Prim. Sch.
Youth Cen.
CALEDONIA ROAD
CABLE STREET
CENTRAL TRADING ESTATE
MONMORE BUSINESS PARK
NEW ENTERPRISE CENTRE
Training Centre
Stow' Heath
BIRMINGHAM RD.
A4123
Learning Disability Services
Recreation Ground
DURBERVILLE RD. IND. EST.
MONMORE PARK IND. EST.
ETTINGSHALL RD.
A4126
Priestfield
THOMPSON AV.
A4123
A459
Playground
PARKFIELD CHALET LAND (CARAVAN PK.)
Phoenix Nursery School
Phoenix Park
WEBNOR INDUSTRIAL ESTATE
Recreation Ground
Playgound
Football Ground
BRONTE
PARKFIELD ROAD
A4039
23
Windsor Nursery School
WATERSIDE IND. EST.
MILLFIELDS RD.
Depot
92
93

A
B
C
D
12
Heath Town
Planetary Rd.
Planetary Industrial Estate
Works
Neachells Lane Industrial Estate
Phoenix Road
Phoenix Road Industrial Estate
Wolverhampton
WV11
395
Fernside Rd.
Key Ind. Park
Waddens Brook
Friesland Drive
Helming
Deans Road
Lewis
Rudge Av.
Drive
Manfield Rd.
Strawberry Lane
Strawberry La. Ind. Est.
Tractor Spares Ind. Est.
Watery Lane
Watery Lane Industrial Estate
Lakeside Prim. Sch.
Lakeside Cl.
Neachell
Hillside Gdns.
Bowmans Rise
99
WV1
Denmore Gds.
Rowlands Av.
Deansfield High School
Neachell Bridge
Neachells Lane
Holman Cl.
Crescent
Beaton Cl.
Lowry Cl.
Hogarth Cl.
Dooley Cl.
Aston Rd.
Oak
Beech
Deansfield Rd.
Teesdale Cl.
Brooklands
Coventry St.
Parade
Hawkley Rd.
Sydenham
Julian
Abingdon
Moseley
Bowker St.
Challenor Av.
Cedar
Sports Ground
Middleton Trad. Est.
Essington
Way
Tyburn Rd.
Pursley Rd.
Willenhall Road
A454
375
553
204
Boundary Cl.
Portobello Cl.
Moseley St.
Evans
Vaughan Rd.
Brook
Millichip Rd.
Wesley Ct.
Vernon Cl.
Plascom
East Park Way
Mayfield Rd.
Selbourne Cr.
Woodstock
Hurstbourne
Cavendish Rd.
Marshall
Uplands Road
Uplands Gro.
Parklands
Lib.
Treynham Road
Wentbridge
Chiltern Dri.
Stow Heath Jun. & Inf. Schs.
Comm. Cen.
Lauder Cl.
Close
Stubbington
Vaughan Road
Alamein
Tobruk Wk.
Arnhem
Barnett Road
Gerrard Rd.
98
17
Tennis Cts.
East Park
Clock Tower
Hollington Rd.
Thornton Rd.
East Park Jun. & Inf. Schs.
Gleaston
Hugh Gaitskell Ct.
Clem Attlee Ct.
Winston Churchill Ct.
View Road
Mount Rd.
Portobello
Bursledon
Park
Warsash
Church
Cherrywood
Lawnside
Green
Hickman
Monmore Green Stadium
Avenue
Stow Lawn
Laburnum Rd.
School
Meadow
Green Pk. Dr.
Walk
Playing Field
Waite
Five
Westfield Av.
Middle
Stowlawn Prim. Sch.
Wholesale Market
Street
Lilac Rd.
Training Centre
Comm. Cen.
Green Park School
Green Park Avenue
Oaklands Grn.
Lanes
Fieldside Walk
Dale Dr.
Moseley Park Sports Cen.
Moseley Park Sch.
Freeman Pl.
Bunkers
Monmore Rd.
Stow Heath
Giffard Rd.
Westfield
Wolseley
Lime Grove
Bilston
Cumberland Road
Holland Rd.
Portway
Bunker Hill
Cullwick
Holloway
Bedford St.
Stow Heath Pl.
Broad Mdw.
Marchant
Fairway
Beach Rd.
Price
Birchdale
Rutland Cres.
Grafton Pl.
Bilston
Lambeth Rd.
City of Wolverhampton Coll. (Wellington Rd. Campus)
Green Lanes
Bilston Cemetery
Best Rd.
Hughes
WV14
Mountford
Queens
Central Avenue
Lansdowne Rd.
Springfield Rd.
5
Road A41 Wellington
Bailey
Hadley Pl.
Haddock Rd.
Southwick Pl.
Villiers Primary Sch.
Priestfield
Brunel Wy.
Junction Rd.
Nelson Av.
Wilkins
Froggatt
Villiers Rd.
Etruria
Barton Ind. Pk.
297
George
John
Wesley
New Street
Hall
Herbert St.
Freeze Land St.
Hindu Temple
Cemetery Rd.
Windsor
Etheridge
Owen Rd.
Nightingale Pl.
Alexandra Pl.
Peascroft La.
Works
Frost
Sidwick Cr.
Victor Cl.
Priest-field St.
Lawley
Prim. Sch.
Play. Fld.
Claremont St.
Eleanor Rd.
Harper Av.
Angela Pl.
Beldray Park
Recreation Ground
6
Priestfield
WV2
B4162
Wolverhampton
Bell St.
Youth Centre
Elm
Dover St.
Leisure Cen.
Pleasant
Ashley
Bilston C of E Prim. Sch.
Talbot Pl.
Albany Cres.
Hickman Park
Broad
The Crescent
Road
Lichfield
Mnt.
Lib.
Bilston Craft Gall & Mus.
Depot
Gas Works
Waterside Ind. Est.
Chestom Road Ind. Est.
Coronation Rd.
Bagnall
Alice St.
Sikh Temple
Bilston Central
Comm. Cen.
Fraser
Prim. Sch.
Millfield
Reliance Trad. Est.
Livingstone
94
Park
Street
24
Oxford St.
395

19
13
25
E
F
G
H
1
2
3
4
5
6
96
97
98
99
WS2
WS10
Willenhall Town FC
Little London
Reflex Industrial Park
Works
Sports Ground
Memorial Park
Willenhall
WV13
Spring Bank
Spring Bank Bridge
Sandbeds Bridge
Monmer Bridge
St. Annes Ind. Est.
Monmer Cl. Ind. Est.
Willenhall Ind. Est.
Elm St. Inf. Sch.
Albion Rd. Jun. Sch.
Chancel Ind. Est.
Cemetery
Croft Indus. Estate
Leisure Centre
St. Giles' C of E Prim. Sch.
Shepwell Green
Shepwell Green Open Space
WILLENHALL
Owen Road Ind. Est.
Willenhall Trading Estate
Neptune Ind. Est.
Criterion Works
Keyway Retail Pk.
Comm. Cen.
St. Thomas More RC Comp. Sch.
Electricity Sub. Sta.
Playing Field
The Lunt
Sports Grd.
Community Centre
Green Acres Primary School
Football Grd.
BILSTON
Pumping Sta.
Rose Park
Darlaston Comm. Sch.
Recreation Ground
Rough Hay Prim. Sch.
Rough Hay
DARLASTON
Wednesbury
RC Prim. Sch.
C of E Prim. Sch.
Alma Ind. Est.
Super-store
Lib.
Woods
Wednesfield Rd.
Walsall Street
Walsall Road
Clarke's La.
A462
B4484
B4464
B4590
A454
A463
A4444
A4038
Black Country Route
Keyway
Bilston Road
Bilston Lane
Owen Road
Armstrong Way
Midland Rd.
Wolverhampton Rd.
Somerford Pl.
New Rd.
Rose Hill
Longacre
Willenhall Rd.
St. Lawrence Way
Pinfold St.
The Green

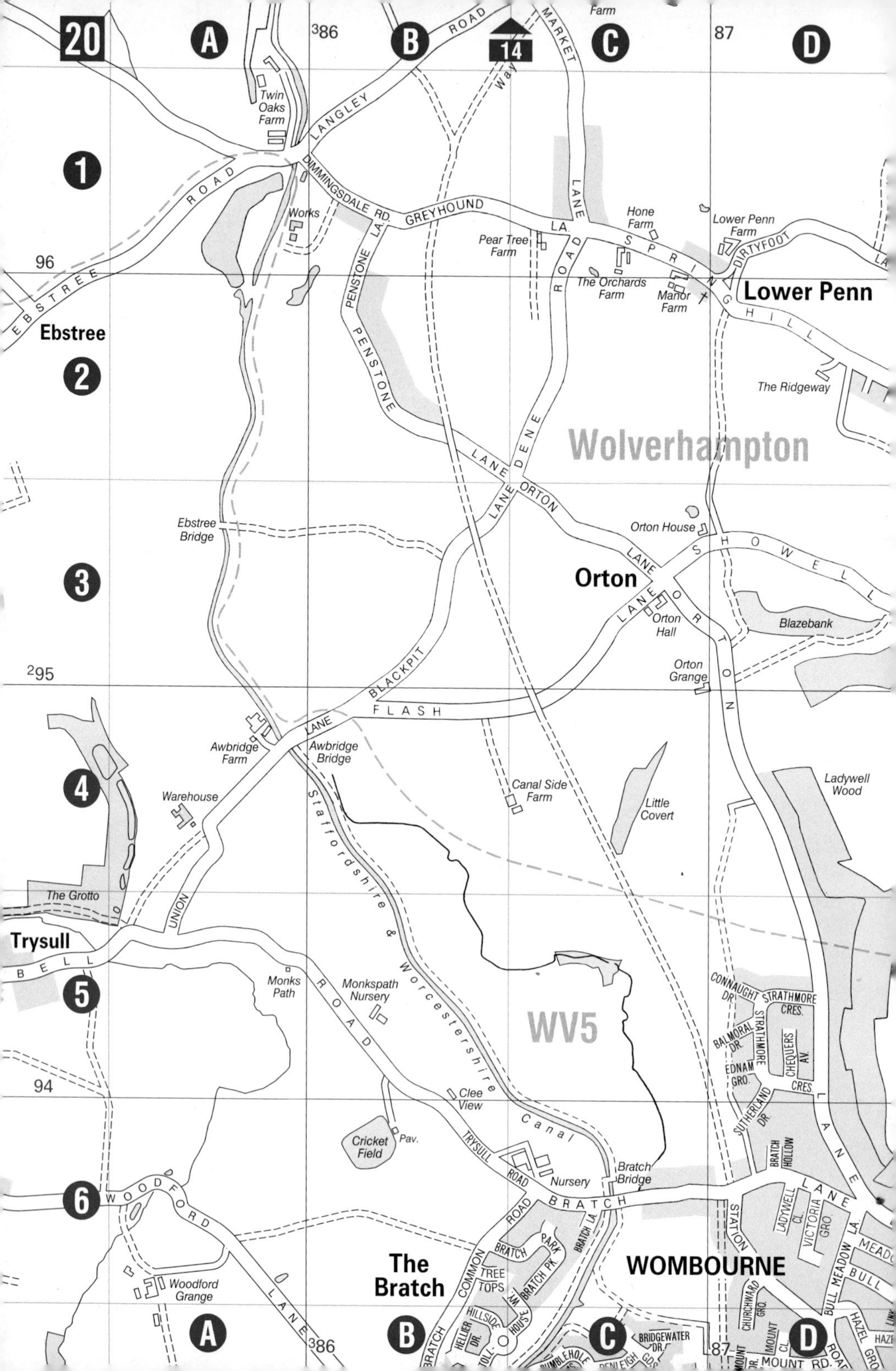
A
386
B
ROAD
14
MARKET
Farm
C
87
D
Twin Oaks Farm
LANGLEY
Way
1
ROAD
DIMMINGSDALE RD.
Works
GREYHOUND
LANE
LA.
Hone Farm
Lower Penn Farm
DIRTYFOOT
Pear Tree Farm
SPRING HILL
96
EBSTREE
The Orchards Farm
Manor Farm
Lower Penn
Ebstree
PENSTONE LA.
PENSTONE
2
The Ridgeway
Wolverhampton
DENE
LANE
ORTON
Ebstree Bridge
Orton House
SHOWELL
3
Orton
LANE
Orton Hall
Blazebank
BLACKPIT
295
Orton Grange
FLASH
LANE
Awbridge Farm
Awbridge Bridge
Warehouse
Canal Side Farm
Ladywell Wood
Little Covert
4
Staffordshire & Worcestershire Canal
The Grotto
UNION
Trysull
BELL
5
Monks Path
Monkspath Nursery
ROAD
CONNAUGHT DR.
STRATHMORE CRES.
BALMORAL DR.
STRATHMORE
EDNAM GRO.
CHEQUERS AV.
WV5
94
Clee View
CRES.
SUTHERLAND DR.
Cricket Field
Pav.
TRYSULL ROAD
Nursery
Bratch Bridge
BRATCH HOLLOW
6
WOODFORD
BRATCH
LANE
STATION
LADYWELL CL.
VICTORIA GRO.
BRATCH LA.
PARK
BRATCH PK.
COMMON ROAD
TREE TOPS
The Bratch
WOMBOURNE
BULL MEADOW LA.
MEADOW
BULL
Woodford Grange
LANE
HILLSIDE
HOUSE
HELLIER DR.
CHURCHWARD GRO.
MOUNT CL.
HAZEL GRO.
A
B
C
D
386
87
BRIDGEWATER
MOUNT RD.
ROAD

21
15
22
E
F
G
H
1
2
3
4
5
6
88
89
96
95
94
Highfields School
Hill Croft Farm
New Croft Farm
Windsor Avenue Playing Fields
Pav.
Penn
Spring Hill
Springdale Jun.& Inf. Schs.
Playing Field
Comm. Cen.
SOUTH STAFFORDSHIRE
WOLVERHAMPTON
Robins Nest Farm
Springhill Poultry Farm
Cricket Ground
Orchard Hill
The Woodlands
PENN HOSPITAL
Penn Hall Sch.
Cemetery
St. Bartholomew's C of E Prim. School
Mount Farm
Turf Tavern
Earlswood
Bradney Wood
Lloyd Farm
WV4
St. Anthonys (West Midlands) Cheshire Home
Light Wood
Lloyd House
Bearnett Farm
Lloyd Home Farm
Lloyd Wood
Brook
Fish Pond
Pear Tree Farm
Nash's Coppice Farm
Nash's Coppice
Lyde
Old Mill Race
Wodehouse Mill Pool
Waterfall
Wodehouse Farm
Bullmeadow Coppice
Dudley
DY3
Baggeridge Wood Farm
The Wodehouse
Weir
Primary School
PENN ROAD
A449
STOURBRIDGE ROAD
WODEHOUSE LANE
A463
WARSTONES DRIVE
SPRINGHILL LANE
BEARNETT LANE
CHAMBERLAINS LANE
VICARAGE ROAD
CHURCH HILL
SEDGLEY ROAD
PENN COMMON RD.
COTSDALE RD.
LLOYD HILL
BRADEN RD.
SWANCOTE
KINVER DR.
STOURTON DR.
WARSTONES CR.
FAIRVIEW RD.
HILSTON AV.
SPRINGHILL GRO.
FOXHILLS RD.
WYNNE CR.
NORTON CL.
FOXLANDS AV.
HOLDEN RD.
BUTTONS FARM RD.
HARTILL RD.
CHANDLER DR.
BEARNETT DR.
MANOR DRIVE
BRENTON RD.
PETERDALE DR.
PENNWOOD LANE
LYTTON AV.
HOLLYBUSH LANE
WYNCHCOMBE AV.
RUTLAND AV.
FANCOURT AV.
SCOTT AV.
WOODHALL RD.
LANCASTER GDNS.
CANTERBURY RD.
REGENT RD.
BUCKLEY RD.
OAKLEY RD.
PINFOLD LANE
LINTON RD.
MASON CRES.
PENNHOUSE AV.
OSBORNE RD.
VIRGINIA DR.
THURSTONE DR.
THE FOLD
BUTTS
WAKELEY HILL
BUNS LANE
WOOD RD.
SCHOOL RD.
SMALLBROOK LANE
WITHYMERE LANE

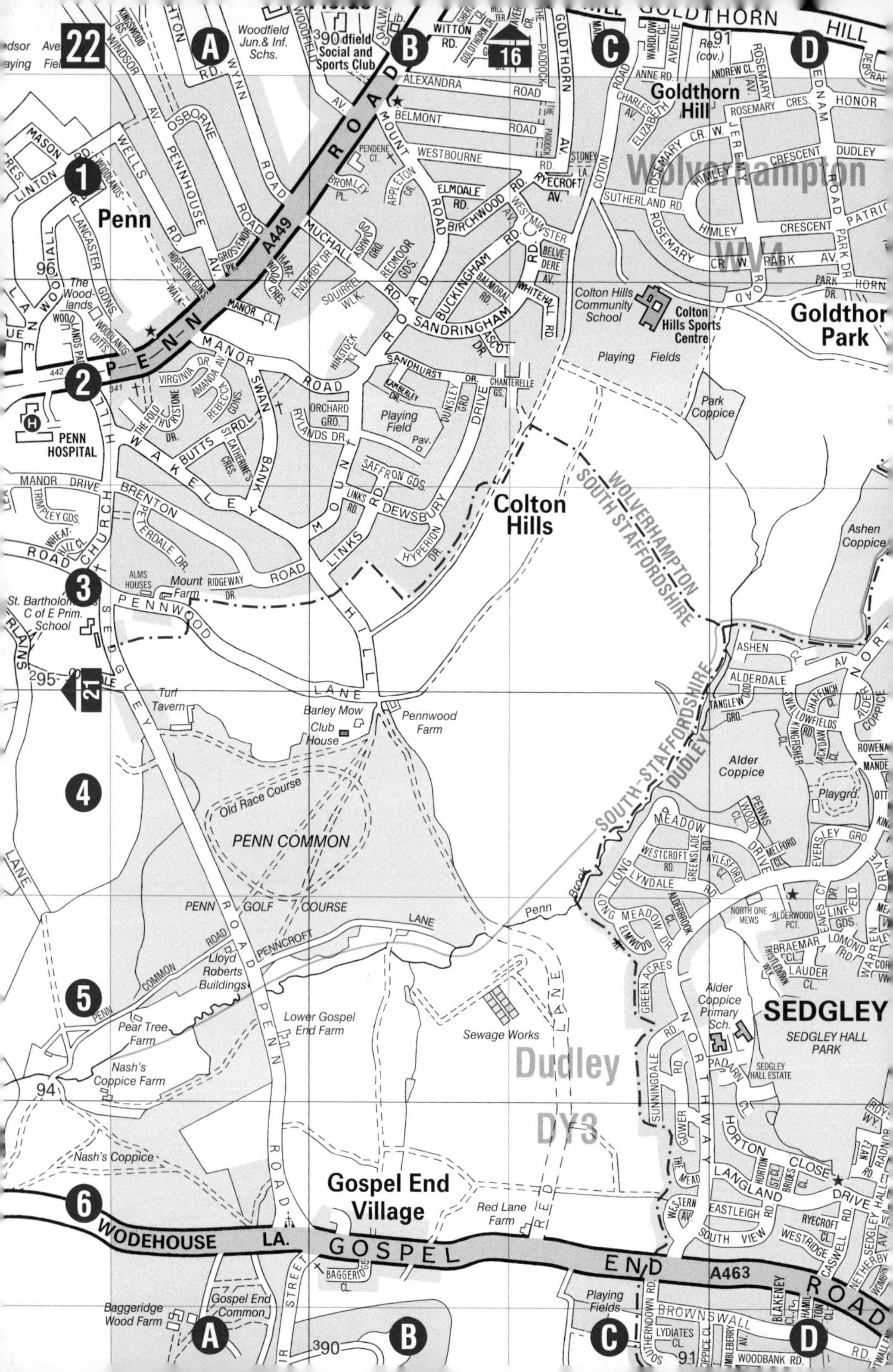

16
21
Penn
Penn Hospital
Woodfield Jun.& Inf. Schs.
Woodfield Social and Sports Club
Goldthorn Hill
Goldthorn Road
Wolverhampton
WV4
Colton Hills Community School
Colton Hills Sports Centre
Goldthorn Park
Playing Fields
Park Coppice
Colton Hills
Wolverhampton South Staffordshire
South Staffordshire Dudley
Ashen Coppice
Alder Coppice
Playgrd.
St. Bartholomew's C of E Prim. School
Alms Houses
Mount Farm
Turf Tavern
Barley Mow Club House
Pennwood Farm
Old Race Course
PENN COMMON
PENN GOLF COURSE
Lloyd Roberts Buildings
Pear Tree Farm
Lower Gospel End Farm
Nash's Coppice Farm
Nash's Coppice
Sewage Works
Penn Brook
Dudley
DY3
Gospel End Village
Red Lane Farm
Alder Coppice Primary Sch.
SEDGLEY
SEDGLEY HALL PARK
Sedgley Hall Estate
Baggeridge Wood Farm
Gospel End Common
Penn Road
A449
Wodehouse La.
Gospel End Road
A463
Mount Road
Manor Road
Wakeley Hill
Church Hill
Sedgley Road
Pennwood Lane
Penncroft Lane
Red Lane
Northway
Swan Bank
Dewsbury Drive
Sandringham Road
Buckingham Road
Alexandra Road
Belmont Road
Westbourne Road
Muchall Road
Penn Common Road
Long Meadow Drive
Green Acres
Horton Close
Langland Drive
Brownswall Road
Woodbank Rd.

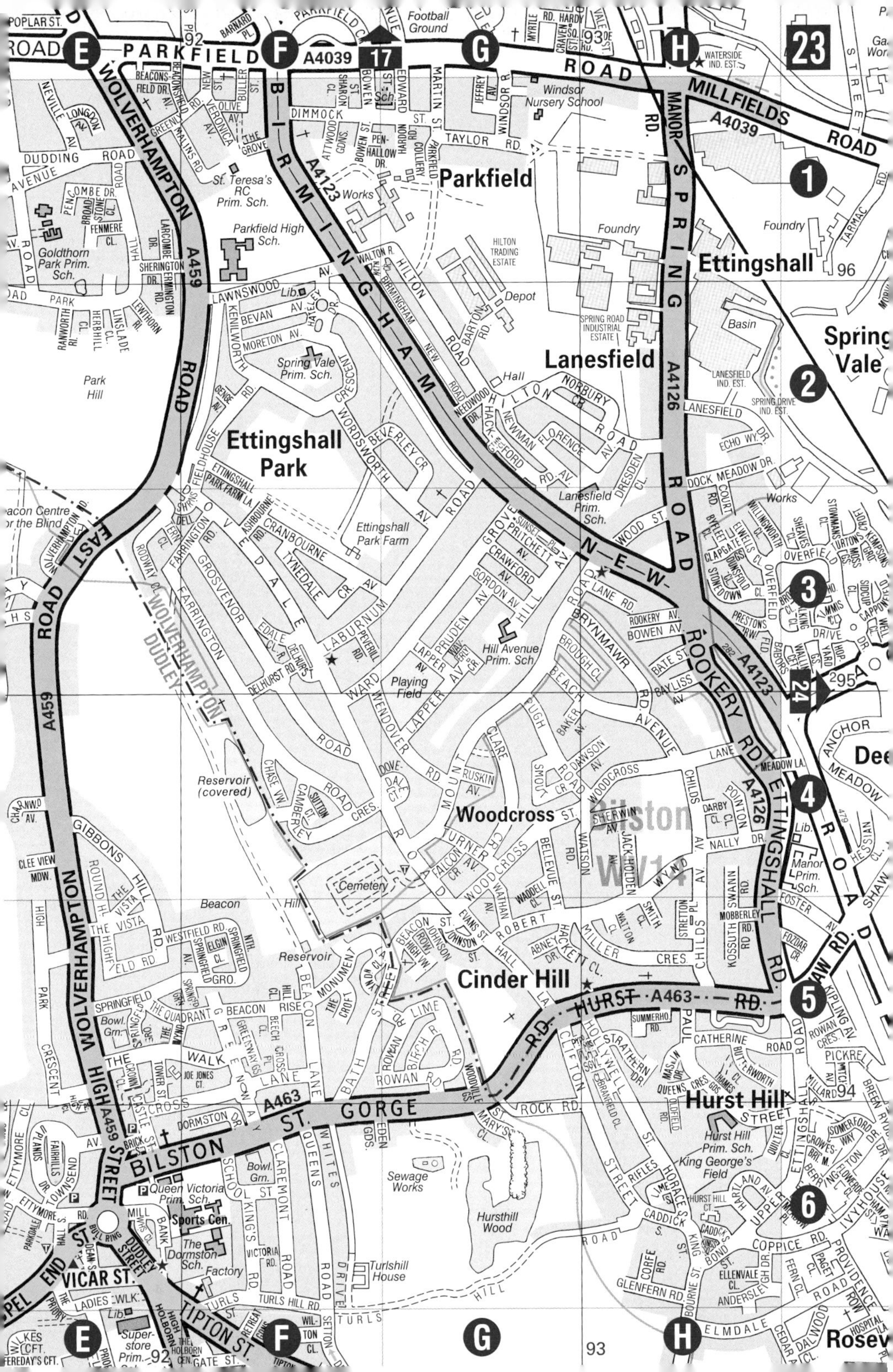

- Parkfield
- Ettingshall
- Ettingshall Park
- Lanesfield
- Spring Vale
- Woodcross
- Cinder Hill
- Hurst Hill
- Bilston
- Roseville

Key roads and features labelled include: Wolverhampton Road, Parkfield Road, Millfields Road (A4039), Birmingham New Road (A4123), Rookery Road (A4126), Ettingshall Road, Hurst Road (A463), Gorge Road, Bilston Street, High Street (A459), East Road (A459), Manor Road, Spring Road, New Road.

Notable locations: Football Ground, Windsor Nursery School, St. Teresa's RC Prim. Sch., Parkfield High Sch., Goldthorn Park Prim. Sch., Spring Vale Prim. Sch., Hilton Trading Estate, Spring Road Industrial Estate, Lanesfield Ind. Est., Lanesfield Prim. Sch., Hill Avenue Prim. Sch., Ettingshall Park Farm, Playing Field, Reservoir (covered), Cemetery, Beacon Centre for the Blind, Manor Prim. Sch., Hurst Hill Prim. Sch., King George's Field, Hursthill Wood, Turlshill House, Sewage Works, Queen Victoria Prim. Sch., The Dormston Sch., Sports Cen., Superstore Prim. Sch., Foundry, Basin, Works, Depot, Hilton, WV14.

Grid references along edges: E, F, G, H (top and bottom); numbered markers 1, 2, 3, 4, 5, 6 (right side); 17, 23, 24 (route/panel numbers).

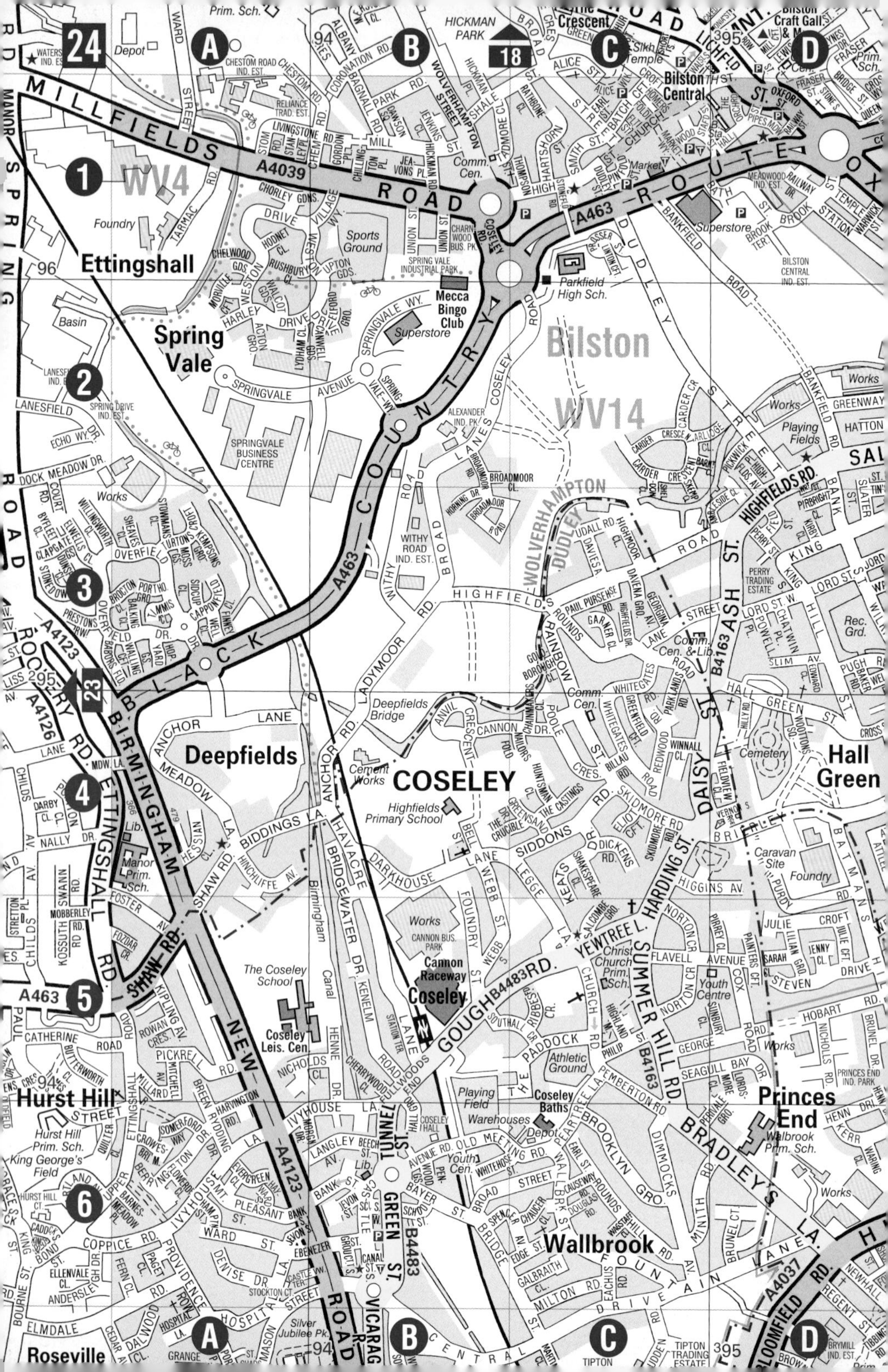

24
18
23
A
B
C
D
1
2
3
4
5
6
WV4
WV14
Ettingshall
Spring Vale
Bilston
Deepfields
COSELEY
Hall Green
Princes End
Hurst Hill
Wallbrook
Roseville
Bilston Central
The Crescent
MILLFIELDS ROAD
A4039
BLACK COUNTRY ROUTE
A463
BIRMINGHAM NEW ROAD
A4123
ETTINGSHALL RD.
A4126
SPRING ROAD
BRADLEY'S LA.
A4037
BLOOMFIELD RD.
GOUGH RD.
B4483
GREEN ST.
TUNNEL ST.
SUMMER HILL RD.
B4163
DAISY ST.
ASH ST.
HIGHFIELDS RD.
WOLVERHAMPTON ST.
DUDLEY STREET
BRIDGE
HICKMAN PARK
Sports Ground
Mecca Bingo Club
Superstore
SPRINGVALE BUSINESS CENTRE
SPRINGVALE AVENUE
Parkfield High Sch.
WITHY ROAD IND. EST.
Highfields Primary School
Cement Works
Deepfields Bridge
The Coseley School
Coseley Leis. Cen.
Cannon Raceway
Coseley
Works
Foundry
Basin
Cemetery
Caravan Site
Athletic Ground
Playing Field
Coseley Baths
Warehouses
Depot
Youth Cen.
Hurst Hill Prim. Sch.
King George's Field
Manor Prim. Sch.
Walbrook Prim. Sch.
Christ Church Prim. Sch.
Youth Centre
Comm. Cen. & Lib.
Silver Jubilee Pk.
TIPTON TRADING ESTATE
PERRY TRADING ESTATE
SPRING VALE INDUSTRIAL PARK
LANESFIELD IND. EST.
SPRING DRIVE IND. EST.
BILSTON CENTRAL IND. EST.
MEADWOOD IND. EST.
PRINCES END IND. PARK
Birmingham Canal
Playing Fields
Rec. Grd.

25
19
E
F
G
H
1
2
3
4
5
6
BILSTON
Moxley
Old Moxley
Woods Bank
Wednesbury
WS10
Lower Bradley
Bradley Lane
Bradley
Loxdale
Ocker Hill
Tipton
DY4
Summer Hill
JUBILEE PARK
A463
A41
A4444
A4038
A4098
A4037
B4163
BLACK COUNTRY NEW ROAD
BLACK-A41-COUNTRY NEW ROAD
HIGH ST.
GREAT BRIDGE ROAD
BILSTON RD.
WEDNESBURY OAK RD.
GOSPEL OAK RD.
LEABROOK RD.
MOXLEY ROAD
PINFOLD ST.
HOLYHEAD ROAD
UPPER CHURCH LA.
Heathfield Bridge
Walsall Canal
Pothouse Bridge
Playing Fields
Bradley Locks
Bradley Bridge
Tup St. Bridge
Wainwright Bridge
Weddell Wynd
Partridge Bridge
Howls Bri.
Moorcroft Wood
Willingsworth High Sch.
Playing Field
Tipton Leisure Centre
Public Open Space
Warehouse
Wednesbury Oak Prim. Sch.
Glebefields Prim. Sch.
St. Martin's C of E Prim. Sch.
Dorothy Purcell Jun. Sch.
Loxdale Prim. Sch.
Moxley Nursy. & Inf. Sch.
Pinfold St. Prim. Sch.
Ocker Hill Jun. Sch.
Jubilee Park Prim. Sch.
Doe Bank Bridge
HOLYHEAD ROAD INDUSTRIAL ESTATE
WEDNESBURY NEW ENTERPRISE CENTRE
AUTOMOTIVE COMPONENTS PARK
THE MAPLE CENTRE
THE WOODS BANK ESTATE
DARLASTON RD. IND. EST.
ATLAS TRADING ESTATE
PHOENIX IND. EST.
STAG IND. EST.
BILSTON KEY IND. EST.
BILSTON IND. EST.
OXFORD ST. IND. EST.
GWS INDUSTRIAL ESTATE
Depot
Bakery
Works
WALSALL
WOLVERHAMPTON
SANDWELL
96
97
94
95

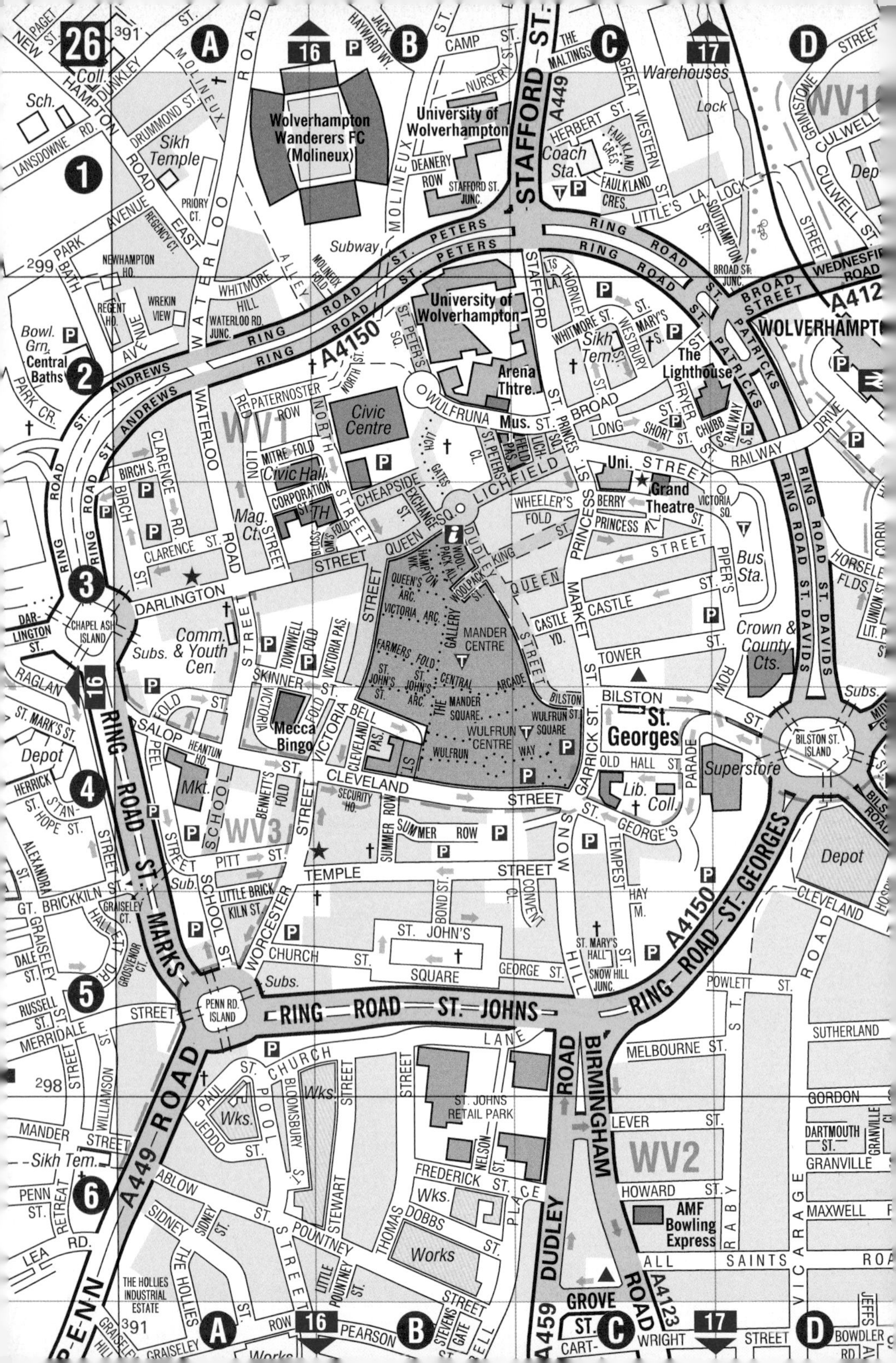
26
A
B
C
D
1
2
3
4
5
6
16
17
391
299
298
Wolverhampton Wanderers FC (Molineux)
University of Wolverhampton
Stafford St.
A449
The Maltings
Warehouses
Lock
WV10
Grimstone Street
Culwell St.
Depot
Camp St.
Nursery St.
Jack Hayward Wy.
Molineux St.
Deanery Row
Stafford St. Junc.
Great Western St.
Herbert St.
Faulkland Cres.
Coach Sta.
Little's La.
Southampton St.
Lock St.
Broad St. Junc.
Wednesfield Road
A4124
Broad Street
Wolverhampton
New Hampton Rd.
Paget St.
Dunkley St.
Coll.
Molineux St.
Sch.
Lansdowne Rd.
Drummond St.
Sikh Temple
Road East
Waterloo Road
Priory Ct.
Park Avenue
Regency Ct.
Bath Avenue
Newhampton Ho.
Regent Ho.
Wrekin View
Whitmore Hill
Waterloo Rd. Junc.
Alley
Molineux Fold
Subway
St. Peters Ring Road
Ring Road St. Andrews
A4150
Bowl. Grn.
Central Baths
Park Cr.
St. Peter's Sq.
North St.
Arena Thtre.
Stafford St.
Lts La.
Thornley St.
Whitmore St.
Sikh Tem.
St. Mary's St.
Westbury St.
The Lighthouse
Fryer St.
Chubb
Railway St.
St. Patricks
Railway Drive
Paternoster Row
Red Lion St.
Waterloo Rd.
Civic Centre
Wulfruna St.
Mus.
Broad St.
Princes Sq.
Long St.
Short St.
Birch St.
Clarence Rd.
WV1
Mitre Fold
Civic Hall
Corporation St.
TH
Cheapside
Exchange St.
Lich Gates
St. Peters Cl.
Giffard Pas.
Lichfield St.
Uni.
Grand Theatre
Victoria Sq.
Mag. Ct.
Bloss. St.
Tom's Fold
Queen Sq.
Wheeler's Fold
Berry St.
Princess Al.
Princess St.
Piper's Row
Bus Sta.
Clarence St.
Darlington St.
Queen Street
Wool. Pack All.
Hampton Wk.
Woolpack St.
King St.
Dudley Street
Market St.
Castle St.
Castle Yd.
Tower St.
Crown & County Cts.
Ring Road St. Davids
Horseley Flds.
Union St.
Lit. Pk.
Corn
Dar-lington St.
Chapel Ash Island
Comm. & Youth Cen.
Subs.
Townwell Fold
Victoria Pas.
Queen's Arc.
Victoria Arc.
Gallery
Mander Centre
Farmers Fold
St. John's St.
St. John's Arc.
Central Arcade
The Mander Square
Wulfrun Square
Wulfrun Centre
Wulfrun Way
Bilston St.
St. Georges
Bilston St. Island
Raglan St.
St. Mark's St.
Depot
Skinner St.
Victoria Fold
Fold St.
Salop St.
Peel St.
Heantun Ho.
Mecca Bingo
Victoria St.
Bell St.
Cleveland Pas.
Mkt.
School St.
Bennett's Fold
Cleveland Street
Old Hall St.
Lib.
Coll.
Garrick St.
Parade
Superstore
Herrick St.
Stanhope St.
Alexandra St.
Ring Road St. Marks
WV3
Security Ho.
Summer Row
St. George's
Tempest St.
Snow Hill
Pitt St.
Temple Street
Convent Cl.
Hay M.
Depot
Cleveland Road
Sub.
Little Brick Kiln St.
Gt. Brickkiln St.
Graiseley Ct.
Hallet Dr.
Graiseley St.
Dale St.
Grosvenor Ct.
Worcester St.
Bond St.
St. John's Square
Church St.
George St.
St. Mary's Hall
Snow Hill Junc.
Ring Road St. Georges
Powlett St.
Subs.
Penn Rd. Island
Ring Road St. Johns
Russell St.
Merridale Street
Lane
Church
Paul St.
Pool St.
Bloomsbury St.
Wks.
Sutherland
Melbourne St.
Birmingham Road
Dudley Road
St. Johns Retail Park
Nelson St.
Gordon
Lever St.
WV2
Williamson St.
Mander Street
Sikh Tem.
Jeddo St.
Dartmouth St.
Granville St.
Granville
Frederick St.
Place
Stewart St.
Howard St.
Maxwell
Penn St.
Retreat St.
Ablow St.
A449 Road
Sidney St.
Pountney Street
Thomas St.
Dobbs St.
Works
AMF Bowling Express
Raby St.
Vicarage Road
Lea Rd.
The Hollies
Little Pountney St.
All Saints Road
The Hollies Industrial Estate
Street
A4123
Penn
Graiseley Hill
Graiseley Row
Pearson St.
Stevens Gate
Grove St.
A459
Cart-wright Street
Jeffs
Bowdler Rd.
Works

INDEX

Including Streets, Places & Areas, Hospitals & Hospices, Industrial Estates,
Selected Flats & Walkways, Stations and Selected Places of Interest.

HOW TO USE THIS INDEX

1. Each street name is followed by its Postcode District and then by its Locality abbreviation(s) and then by its map reference;
e.g. **Abbeyfield Rd.** WV10: Bush . . . .4F **5** is in the WV10 Postcode District and the Bushbury Locality and is to be found in square 4F on page **5**.
The page number is shown in bold type.

2. A strict alphabetical order is followed in which Av., Rd., St., etc. (though abbreviated) are read in full and as part of the street name;
e.g. **Ash Cl.** appears after **Ashburn Gro.** but before **Ashen Cl.**

3. Streets and a selection of flats and walkways too small to be shown on the maps, appear in the index with the thoroughfare to which it is connected shown
in brackets; e.g. **Albert Ho.** WS10: Darl . . . .6H **19** (off Factory St.)

4. Addresses that are in more than one part are referred to as not continuous.

5. Places and areas are shown in the index in **BLUE TYPE** and the map reference is to the actual map square in which the town centre or area is located
and not to the place name shown on the map; e.g. **ASHMOOR LAKE 5G 13**

6. An example of a selected place of interest is **Arena Theatre. . . . .2D 16 (2B 26)**

7. An example of a station is **Bilbrook Station (Rail) 6E 3**

8. An example of a hospital or hospice is **COMPTON HOSPICE 2F 15**

9. Map references shown in brackets; e.g **Ablow St.** WV2: Wolv . . . .4D **16** (6A **26**) refer to entries that also appear on the large scale page **26**.

GENERAL ABBREVIATIONS

All. : Alley	**E.** : East	**La.** : Lane	**Rd.** : Road
Arc. : Arcade	**Ent.** : Enterprise	**Lit.** : Little	**Shop.** : Shopping
Av. : Avenue	**Est.** : Estate	**Lwr.** : Lower	**Sth.** : South
Bri. : Bridge	**Fld.** : Field	**Mnr.** : Manor	**Sq.** : Square
Bus. : Business	**Flds.** : Fields	**Mdw.** : Meadow	**St.** : Street
Cvn. : Caravan	**Gdns.** : Gardens	**Mdws.** : Meadows	**Ter.** : Terrace
Cen. : Centre	**Ga.** : Gate	**M.** : Mews	**Twr.** : Tower
Chu. : Church	**Gt.** : Great	**Mt.** : Mount	**Trad.** : Trading
Cir. : Circus	**Grn.** : Green	**Mus.** : Museum	**Up.** : Upper
Cl. : Close	**Gro.** : Grove	**Nth.** : North	**Va.** : Vale
Comn. : Common	**Hgts.** : Heights	**Pde.** : Parade	**Vw.** : View
Cotts. : Cottages	**Ho.** : House	**Pk.** : Park	**Wlk.** : Walk
Ct. : Court	**Ho's.** : Houses	**Pas.** : Passage	**W.** : West
Cres. : Crescent	**Ind.** : Industrial	**Pl.** : Place	**Yd.** : Yard
Cft. : Croft	**Info.** : Information	**Pct.** : Precinct	
Dr. : Drive	**Junc.** : Junction	**Ri.** : Rise	

LOCALITY ABBREVIATIONS

Bilb : **Bilbrook**	**Darl** : **Darlaston**	**Oxl** : **Oxley**	**Tres** : **Trescott**
Bils : **Bilston**	**Ess** : **Essington**	**Pend** : **Pendeford**	**Try** : **Trysull**
B'frd : **Brinsford**	**E'shll** : **Ettingshall**	**Penn** : **Penn**	**Wals** : **Walsall**
Bush : **Bushbury**	**F'stne** : **Featherstone**	**Pert** : **Perton**	**W'bry** : **Wednesbury**
Cod : **Codsall**	**F'hses** : **Fordhouses**	**Sed** : **Sedgley**	**Wed** : **Wednesfield**
Cod W : **Codsall Wood**	**Gt Wyr** : **Great Wyrley**	**Seis** : **Seisdon**	**W'hall** : **Willenhall**
Cose : **Coseley**	**Lwr G** : **Lower Gornal**	**Share** : **Shareshill**	**Wolv** : **Wolverhampton**
Coven : **Coven**	**Lwr P** : **Lower Penn**	**S Hth** : **Slade Heath**	**Wom** : **Wombourne**
Cov H : **Coven Heath**	**Mox** : **Moxley**	**Tett** : **Tettenhall**	
C Grn : **Cross Green**	**Oaken** : **Oaken**	**Tip** : **Tipton**	

A

Aaron Manby Ct. DY4: Tip 6E 25
Abbeyfield Rd. WV10: Bush 4F 5
Abbots Way WV3: Wolv 3H 15
Aberford Cl. WV12: W'hall 6H 13
Abingdon Cl. WV1: Wolv 2A 18
Abingdon Rd. WV1: Wolv 2A 18
Ablow St. WV2: Wolv 4D 16 (6A 26)
Abney Dr. WV14: Cose 5G 23
Acacia Cres. WV8: Bilb 4E 3
Accord M. WS10: Darl 5H 19
Ackleton Gdns. WV3: Wolv 5A 16
Acorn Gro. WV8: Cod 6B 2
Acorn Rd. WV11: Wed 1F 13
Acorn St. WV13: W'hall 6H 19
Acre Ri. WV12: W'hall 5G 13
Acres, The WV3: Wolv 3F 15
Acton Gro. WV14: Bils 2A 24
Adams Cl. DY4: Tip 5E 25
Adams Rd. WV3: Wolv 5F 15
Ada Wrighton Cl. WV12: W'hall . .3H 13
Addenbrooke St. WS10: Darl 4H 19
Addenbrook Way DY4: Tip 6H 25
Addison Gro. WV11: Wed 1A 12
Addison Pl. WV14: Bils 5F 19
Addison Rd. WV3: Wolv 4A 16
Adelaide Wlk. WV2: Wolv 4F 17
Adey Rd. WV11: Wed 2E 13
Adwalton Rd. WV6: Pert 1C 14
Ainsworth Rd. WV10: Bush 3F 5
Aintree Rd. WV10: F'hses 4E 5
Alamein Rd. WV13: W'hall 3D 18
Albany Cres. WV14: Bils 6B 18
Albany Gro. WV11: Ess 1H 13
Albany Rd. WV1: Wolv 2C 16
Albert Clarke Dr. WV12: W'hall . .3H 13
Albert Cl. WV8: Cod 4B 2

Albert Ho. WS10: Darl 6H 19
(off Factory St.)
Albert Rd. WV6: Wolv 1A 16
Albert St. DY4: Tip 6E 25
Albion Av. WV13: W'hall 2H 19
Albion Rd. WV13: W'hall 2G 19
Albion St. WV1: Wolv 2E 17
WV13: W'hall 2H 19
WV14: Bils 6D 18
Alcester Dr. WV13: W'hall 3C 18
Alderbrook Cl. DY3: Sed 5C 22
Alder Coppice DY3: Sed 4D 22
Alder Dale WV3: Wolv 3H 15
Alderdale Av. DY3: Sed 3D 22
Alderford Cl. WV8: Pend 2A 10
Aldersley Av. WV6: Tett 3H 9
Aldersley Cl. WV6: Tott 3A 10
Aldersley High School Sports Cen.
. . . . .1G 9
Aldersley Leisure Village 4A 10
Aldersley Rd. WV6: Tett 5H 9
Aldersley Stadium 4A 10
Alderton Dr. WV3: Wolv 4H 15
Alderwood Pct. DY3: Sed 5D 22
Aldwyck Dr. WV3: Wolv 4D 14
Alexander Ind. Pk.
WV14: Bils 2B 24
Alexander Rd. WV8: Bilb 5F 3
Alexandra Pl. WV14: Bils 6C 18
Alexandra Rd. WV4: Penn 1B 22
Alexandra St.
WV3: Wolv 3C 16 (4A 26)
Alfred Squire Rd. WV11: Wed . . .5B 12
Alfred St. WS10: Darl 1H 25
Alice St. WV14: Bils 6C 18
Alice Wlk. WV14: Bils 1C 24
Alison Cl. DY4: Tip 4F 25
Allcock St. DY4: Tip 6H 25
Allen Dr. WS10: Darl 6H 19

Allen Rd. DY4: Tip 5E 25
WV6: Wolv 1A 16
Allen's Cl. WV12: W'hall 5G 13
Alleston Rd. WV10: Bush 6E 5
Alleston Wlk. WV10: Bush 6E 5
All Saints' Rd.
WV2: Wolv 4E 17 (6C 26)
Alma Av. DY4: Tip 6F 25
Alma Ind. Est. WS10: Darl 6H 19
Almar Ct. WV8: Pend 1A 10
Alma St. WS10: Darl 6H 19
WV10: Wolv 1G 17
WV13: W'hall 2G 19
Alma Works WS10: Darl 1H 25
Almond Gro. WV6: Wolv 6D 10
Alms Ho's. WV4: Penn 3A 22
Alpine Way WV3: Wolv 2F 15
Alton Av. WV12: W'hall 6G 13
Alton Cl. WV10: Bush 5F 5
Alverstoke Cl. WV9: Pend 6B 4
Amanda Av. WV4: Penn 2A 22
Amberwood Cl. WS2: Wals 1H 19
Ambleside Cl. WV14: Bils 3D 24
Ambleside Gro. WV12: W'hall . . .1G 13
Ambrose Cl. WV13: W'hall 2D 18
Ames Rd. WS10: Darl 5H 19
AMF Bowling
Oxley 4D 10
Wolverhampton . . .4E 17 (6C 26)
Amos Av. WV11: Wed 3A 12
Amos La. WV11: Wed 3B 12
Anchor La. WV14: Cose 4A 24
(not continuous)
Anchor Rd. WV14: Cose 4B 24
Andersleigh Dr. WV14: Cose 6H 23
Anders Sq. WV6: Pert 6B 8
Andrew Rd. DY4: Tip 5F 25
Angela Pl. WV14: Bils 6C 18
Angel St. WV13: W'hall 2F 19

Annan Av. WV10: Bush 3F 11
Anne Gro. DY4: Tip 5G 25
Anne Rd. WV4: Penn 6C 16
Ann St. WV13: W'hall 1G 19
Anslow Gdns. WV11: Wed 1E 13
Anson Ct. WV6: Pert 5B 8
Anston Way WV11: Wed 3C 12
Anvil Cres. WV14: Cose 4B 24
Appleby Gdns. WV11: Ess 6H 7
Appleton Cres. WV4: Penn 1B 22
Appletree Dr. WV6: Wolv 5D 10
Arden Pl. WV14: Bils 2G 25
Arena Theatre 2D 16 (2B 26)
Argil Cl. WV11: Wed 2C 12
Argyle Rd. WV2: Wolv 6C 16
Argyll Ho. WV1: Wolv 6D 10
Arley Gro. WV4: Penn 1G 21
Arlidge Cl. WV14: Bils 2C 24
Armstead Rd. WV9: Pend 5A 4
Armstrong Dr. WV6: Wolv 5B 10
Armstrong Way
WV13: W'hall 4G 19
Arnhem Cl. WV11: Wed 2A 12
Arnhem Rd. WV13: W'hall 4D 18
Arps Rd. WV8: Cod 5C 2
Arrow Ind. Est. WV12: W'hall . . .4H 13
Arthur St. WV2: Wolv 6D 16
WV14: Bils 6C 18
Arundel Gro. WV6: Pert 1C 14
Arundel Rd. WV10: Oxl 6C 4
Arundel St. WV13: W'hall 3H 13
Ascot Dr. WV4: Penn 2B 22
Ashbourne Rd. WV1: Wolv 1H 17
WV4: E'shll 3F 23
Ashburn Gro. WV13: W'hall 2H 19
Ash Cl. WV8: Bilb 5D 2
Ashen Cl. DY3: Sed 3D 22
Ashenden Ri. WV3: Wolv 3H 14
Ashfield Gro. WV10: F'hses 5D 4

Ashfield Rd.—Brailsford Cl.

Ashfield Rd. WV3: Wolv 2G 15
WV10: F'hses 5D 4
WV14: Bils 4F 25
Ash Hill WV3: Wolv 3G 15
Ashley Gdns. WV8: Cod 4C 2
Ashley Mt. WV6: Tett 5G 9
Ashley Rd. WV4: Penn 1H 21
Ashley St. WV14: Bils 6D 18
ASHMOOR LAKE 5G 13
Ashmore Av. WV11: Wed 2F 13
Ashmore Lake Ind. Est.
WV12: W'hall 6G 13
Ashmore Lake Rd.
WV12: W'hall 6G 13
Ashmore Lake Way
WV12: W'hall 6G 13
ASHMORE PARK 1F 13
Ash St. WV3: Wolv 3B 16
WV14: Bils 3D 24
Ashtree Gro. WV14: Bils 3G 25
Ashwells Gro. WV9: Pend 6B 4
Ashwood Gro. WV4: Penn 1B 22
Aspen Way WV3: Wolv 3B 16
Astbury Cl. WV1: Wolv 3H 17
Aster Wlk. WV9: Pend 5B 4
Astley Pl. WV2: Wolv 6E 17
Aston Cl. WV14: Bils 2G 25
Aston Rd. WV13: W'hall 2D 18
Aston St. WV3: Wolv 4B 16
Astoria Cl. WV12: W'hall 1H 13
Astoria Gdns. WV12: W'hall 1H 13
Athelstan Gro. WV6: Pert 5C 8
Atherstone Rd. WV1: Wolv 2A 18
Atlantic Ct. *WV13: W'hall* *3F 19*
(off Cheapside)
Atlas Cft. WV10: Oxl 4D 10
Atlas Trad. Est. WV14: Bils 4E 25
Attlee Cres. WV14: Bils 4D 24
Attwell Pk. WV3: Wolv 5G 15
Attwell Rd. DY4: Tip 5E 25
Attwood Gdns. WV4: E'shll 1F 23
Auden Ct. WV6: Pert 6C 8
Audlem Wlk. WV10: Wolv 5H 11
Austin St. WV6: Wolv 6C 10
Automotive Components Pk.
WS10: W'bry 3H 25
Avenue, The WV3: Wolv 4E 15
WV4: Penn 2H 21
WV10: F'stne 1A 6
WV10: Wolv 5G 11
Avenue Rd. WV3: Wolv 2H 15
WV14: Cose 6B 24
Avington Cl. DY3: Sed 6E 23
Avion Cen. WV6: Wolv 6B 10
Avon Cl. WV6: Pert 1C 14
Avondale Rd. WV6: Wolv 1A 16
Avon Dr. WV13: W'hall 2H 19
Aylesford Cl. DY3: Sed 4D 22
Ayrton Cl. WV6: Pert 6D 8
Azalea Cl. WV8: Bilb 5E 3

B

Babors Fld. WV14: Cose 3H 23
Babworth Cl. WV9: Pend 6B 4
Backhouse La. WV11: Wed 6B 12
Bader Rd. WV6: Pert 1B 14
Baggeridge Cl. DY3: Sed 6B 22
Baggott St. WV2: Wolv 5D 16
Bagnall Rd. WV14: Bils 1B 24
Bagnall St. DY4: Tip 5H 25
Bagridge Cl. WV3: Wolv 4E 15
Bagridge Rd. WV3: Wolv 4E 15
Bailey Rd. WV14: Bils 5A 18
Bailey St. WV1: Wolv 2F 17
Baker Av. WV14: Cose 4G 23
Baker Rd. WV14: Bils 3D 24
Bakers Gdns. WV8: Cod 4B 2
Bakers Way WV8: Cod 4B 2
Baldwin St. WV14: Bils 2E 25
Balfour Ct. *WV6: Wolv* *6A 10*
(off Balfour Cres.)
Balfour Cres. WV6: Wolv 6A 10
Balking Cl. WV14: Cose 3A 24
Balliol Bus. Pk.
WV9: Pend 5G 3
Ball La. WV10: Cov H 2D 4
Balmain Cres. WV11: Wed 2A 12
Balmoral Dr. WV5: Wom 5D 20
WV12: W'hall 3G 13
Balmoral Rd. WV4: Penn 1B 22
Bamber Cl. WV3: Wolv 4H 15
Bamford Rd. WV3: Wolv 4B 16
Baneberry Dr.
WV10: F'stne 1A 6
Banfield Av. WS10: Darl 5H 19
Banfield Rd. WS10: Darl 2H 25
Bankfield Rd. DY4: Tip 6H 25
WV14: Bils 1C 24
(not continuous)
Banks St. WV13: W'hall 2F 19
Bank St. WV10: Wolv 5F 11
WV14: Bils 3D 24
WV14: Cose 6A 24
Bannington Ct. WV12: W'hall 6H 13
Bannister Rd. WS10: W'bry 4H 25
Banstead Cl. WV2: Wolv 5F 17
Bantock Av. WV3: Wolv 4A 16
Bantock Ct. WV3: Wolv 4H 15
Bantock Gdns. WV3: Wolv 3H 15
Bantock House Mus. 3A 16
Barbel Dr. WV10: Wolv 6H 11
Barclay Ct. WV3: Wolv 2B 16
Barcroft WV13: W'hall 1G 19
Bardwell Cl. WV8: Pend 2A 10
Barford Cl. WS10: Darl 4H 19
Bargate Dr. WV6: Wolv 6B 10
Bargery Rd. WV11: Wed 1F 13
Barley Cl. WV8: Pend 1H 9
Barley Cft. WV6: Pert 1A 14
Barmouth Cl. WV12: W'hall 4H 13
Barnaby Sq. WV10: Bush 4G 5
Barnard Pl. WV2: Wolv 6F 17
Barnard Rd. WV11: Wed 1E 13
Barnesmeadow Pl.
WV14: Cose 6A 24
Barnett Cl. WV14: Bils 2C 24
Barnett Rd. WV13: W'hall 3D 18
Barn Farm Cl. WV14: Bils 5F 19
Barnfield Rd. WV1: Wolv 2H 17
Barn Grn. WV3: Wolv 5A 16
Barnhurst La. WV8: Bilb, Pend 5G 3
Barnwood Rd. WV8: Pend 1H 9
Barrington Cl. WV10: Oxl 1D 10
Bartlett Cl. DY4: Tip 5G 25
Barton Ind. Pk. WV14: Bils 5D 18
Barton Rd. WV4: E'shll 2G 23
Bassett Cl. WV4: Penn 6F 15
WV12: W'hall 6H 13
Batch Cft. WV14: Bils 1C 24
Bates Gro. WV10: Wolv 5H 11
Bate St. WV4: E'shll 3H 23
Bath Av. WV1: Wolv 2C 16 (1A 26)
Bath Rd. WV1: Wolv 2C 16
Bath St. DY3: Sed 5F 23
WV1: Wolv 3F 17
WV13: W'hall 3G 19
WV14: Bils 1D 24
Batmans Hill Rd. DY4: Tip 4D 24
WV14: Bils 4D 24
Bayer St. WV14: Cose 6B 24
Bayley Cres. WS10: Darl 4H 19
Bayleys La. DY4: Tip 6H 25
Baylis Av. WV11: Wed 2E 13
Bayliss Av. WV4: E'shll 3H 23
Bayliss Cl. WV14: Bils 5B 18
Baynton Rd. WV12: W'hall 3H 13
Bayston Av. WV3: Wolv 4H 15
Beach Av. WV14: Cose 3G 23
Beach Rd. WV14: Bils 5C 18
Beacon La. DY3: Sed 5F 23
Beacon Pas. *DY3: Sed* *6E 23*
(off High St.)
Beacon Ri. DY3: Sed 5F 23
Beacon Rd. WV12: W'hall 2H 13
Beaconsfield Av. WV4: E'shll 6E 17
Beaconsfield Dr. WV4: E'shll 6E 17
Beacon St. WV14: Cose 5G 23
Bealeys Av. WV11: Wed 2B 12
Bealeys Fold *WV11: Wed* *5C 12*
(off Nicholls Fold)
Bearnett Dr. WV4: Penn 4F 21
Bearnett La. WV4: Lwr P 5E 21
WV5: Wom 5E 21
Beaton Cl. WV13: W'hall 2D 18
Beatty Ho. DY4: Tip 6F 25
Beaver Cl. WV11: Wed 5E 13
Bebington Cl. WV8: Pend 2A 10
Beccles Dr. WV13: W'hall 4E 19
Beckbury Av. WV4: Penn 1F 21
Beckett St. WV14: Bils 6D 18
Beckminster Rd. WV3: Wolv 5A 16
Bedford Ho. WV1: Wolv 6D 10
Bedford St. WV1: Wolv 5A 18
Beech Cl. DY3: Sed 5F 23
WV10: Oxl 2C 10
Beech Cres. DY4: Tip 6H 25
Beechcroft Pl. WV10: Oxl 3D 10
Beeches, The WV1: Wolv 1B 16
Beech Gdns. WV8: Cod 6C 2
Beech Rd. WV10: Oxl 2C 10
WV13: W'hall 2D 18
Beech St. WV14: Cose 6B 24
Beech Tree Av. WV11: Wed 2B 12
Beechwood Av. WV11: Wed 2A 12
Beechwood Ct. WV6: Tett 1F 15
Beechwood Dr. WV6: Tett 2D 14
Bee La. WV10: F'hses 5E 5
Beldray Pk. WV14: Bils 6D 18
Beldray Rd. WV14: Bils 6D 18
Belfry, The WV6: Pert 6A 8
Belgrade Rd. WV10: Oxl 1C 10
Belinda Cl. WV13: W'hall 1E 19
Bellamy La. WV11: Wed 3B 12
Bell Av. WV13: W'hall 2F 19
Bell Cl. WS10: Darl 5H 19
Bellencroft Gdns. WV3: Wolv 5F 15
Bellevue Rd. WV14: Bils 4F 25
Bellevue St. WV14: Cose 4G 23
Bellflower Cl. WV10: F'stne 1H 5
Bellman Cl. WS10: Darl 5H 19
Bell Pl. WV2: Wolv 4D 16 (6B 26)
Bell Rd. WV5: Try 5A 20
Bell St. WS10: Darl 5H 19
WV1: Wolv 3D 16 (4B 26)
WV14: Bils 6B 18
WV14: Cose 4B 24
Belmont Gdns. WV14: Bils 2F 25
Belmont Rd. WV4: Penn 1B 22
Belmont St. WV14: Bils 2F 25
Belton Av. WV11: Wed 1A 12
Belvedere Av. WV4: Penn 1C 22
Belvedere Gdns. WV6: Tett 3H 9
Belvide Gdns. WV8: Cod 4C 2
Bembridge Cl. WV12: W'hall 2G 13
Bencroft WV8: Bilb 4E 3
Bennett's Fold
WV3: Wolv 3D 16 (4A 26)
Benson Av. WV4: Penn 1D 22
Benson Cl. WV6: Pert 5B 8
Bentley Bridge Leisure Pk. 6A 12
Bentley Bri. Way WV11: Wed 6A 12
Bentley Dr. WV8: Cod 4C 2
Bentley La. WV12: W'hall 5H 13
Bentley Rd. WV10: Bush 6F 5
Berkeley Cl. WV6: Pert 1C 14
Berrington Dr. WV14: Cose 6A 24
Berry Av. WS10: Darl 1G 25
Berry St. WV1: Wolv 2E 17 (3C 26)
Bertram Cl. DY4: Tip 5H 25
Best Rd. WV14: Bils 5C 18
Betjeman Pl. WV10: Bush 1H 11
Bettany Glade WV10: Bush 4F 5
Bevan Av. WV4: E'shll 2F 23
Bevan Cl. WV14: Bils 6E 19
Beverley Cres. WV4: E'shll 2G 23
Beverston Rd. DY4: Tip 4G 25
WV6: Pert 6D 8
Bewdley Dr. WV1: Wolv 2A 18
Bhylls Cres. WV3: Wolv 5F 15
Bhylls La. WV3: Wolv 4E 15
Bibbey's Grn. WV10: Bush 4G 5
Bickford Rd. WV10: Wolv 5G 11
Bickley Rd. WV14: Bils 5F 19
Biddings La. WV14: Cose 4A 24
Biddlestone Pl. WS10: Darl 5G 19
Biggin Cl. WV6: Pert 5B 8
Bilboe Rd. WV14: Bils 3E 25
BILBROOK 4E 3
Bilbrook Ct. WV8: Bilb 5E 3
Bilbrook Gro. WV8: Bilb 5E 3
Bilbrook Ho. WV8: Bilb 5E 3
Bilbrook Rd. WV8: Bilb, Cod 4D 2
(not continuous)
Bilbrook Station (Rail) 6E 3
Billau Rd. WV14: Cose 4C 24
Billy Buns La. WV5: Wom 6D 20
Billy Wright Cl. WV4: Penn 6H 15
BILSTON 1E 25
Bilston Central Ind. Est.
WV14: Bils 1D 24
Bilston Central (MM) 1C 24
Bilston Craft Gallery & Mus. 6D 18
Bilston Ind. Est. WV14: Bils 1F 25
Bilston Key Ind. Est.
WV14: Bils 1E 25
Bilston Leisure Cen. 6C 18
Bilston Rd. DY4: Tip 4G 25
WV2: Wolv 3F 17 (4D 26)
WV13: W'hall 5F 19
Bilston St. DY3: Sed 6E 23
WS10: Darl 6H 19
(not continuous)
WV1: Wolv 3E 17 (4C 26)
WV13: W'hall 3F 19
Bilston St. Island
WV1: Wolv 3E 17 (4D 26)
Bingley Ent. Cen. *WV3: Wolv* *4B 16*
(off Norfolk Rd.)
Bingley St. WV3: Wolv 4B 16
Birch Ct. WV1: Wolv 6D 10
Birchdale WV14: Bils 5C 18
Birches Av. WV8: Bilb 1F 9
Birches Barn Av. WV3: Wolv 5A 16
Birches Barn Rd. WV3: Wolv 4A 16
Birches Pk. Rd. WV8: Cod 6D 2
Birches Ri. WV13: W'hall 3F 19
Birches Rd. WV8: Bilb 6D 2
Birchfield Av. WV6: Tett 4E 9
Birchfields Rd. WV12: W'hall 5F 13
Birchglade WV3: Wolv 3G 15
Birch Rd. DY3: Sed 5G 23
WV11: Wed 1E 13
Birch St. WV1: Wolv 2D 16 (2A 26)
Birchwood Cl. WV11: Ess 5F 7
Birchwood Rd. WV4: Penn 1B 22
Birkdale Cl. WV1: Wolv 2H 17
Birmingham New Rd.
WV4: E'shll 1F 23
WV14: Cose 1F 23
Birmingham Rd.
WV2: Wolv 3E 17 (5C 26)
Birmingham St. WV13: W'hall 2G 19
Bissell St. WV14: Bils 1E 25
Bi-Tec Ind. Pk. WV1: Wolv 3H 17
Bittell Cl. WV10: Bush 4F 5
Bitterne Dr. WV6: Wolv 6B 10
Blackbrook Way WV10: Bush 4F 5
Blackburn Av. WV6: Tett 3H 9
Black Country New Rd.
DY4: Tip 6H 25
WS10: Darl, W'bry 2G 25
WV14: Bils 6F 19
Black Country Route
WV13: W'hall 5G 19
WV14: Cose, Bils 3A 24
Blackhalve La.
WV11: Wed, Ess 2A 12
Blackham Rd. WV11: Wed 2E 13
Blackpit La. WV4: Lwr P 3B 20
Blackwood Av. WV11: Wed 2A 12
Blakeley Av. WV6: Tett 3A 10
Blakeley Ri. WV6: Tett 3A 10
Blakeley Wood Rd. DY4: Tip 6H 25
Blakeney Cl. DY3: Sed 6D 22
BLAKENHALL 5D 16
Blakenhall Gdns. WV2: Wolv 5D 16
Blakenhall Ind. Est. WV2: Wolv 5C 16
Blanefield WV8: Pend 6H 3
Blaydon Rd. WV9: Pend 6B 4
Blenheim Rd. WV12: W'hall 4G 13
Blockall WS10: Darl 5H 19
Blockall Cl. WS10: Darl 6H 19
Bloomfield Dr. WV12: W'hall 1H 13
Bloomfield Ter. DY4: Tip 6D 24
Bloomsbury St.
WV2: Wolv 4D 16 (5A 26)
Blossom's Fold
WV1: Wolv 2D 16 (3B 26)
Bloxwich Rd. Nth.
WV12: W'hall 4H 13
Bloxwich Rd. Sth.
WV13: W'hall 1F 19
Bluebell Cres. WV11: Wed 5C 12
Bluebird Trad. Est. WV10: Wolv 5F 11
Blythe Gdns. WV8: Cod 4C 2
Bodiam Ct. WV6: Pert 1D 14
Bognop Rd. WV11: Ess 4B 6
Bolton Ct. DY4: Tip 6H 25
Bolton Rd. WV11: Wed 5B 12
Bond St. WV2: Wolv 3D 16 (5B 26)
WV14: Cose 6H 23
Bonny Stile La. WV11: Wed 4A 12
Bonville Gdns. WV10: Bush 4F 5
Booth St. WS10: Darl 4H 19
Borden Cl. WV8: Pend 2A 10
Borrow St. WV13: W'hall 1F 19
Boscobel Cres. WV1: Wolv 6D 10
Boswell Cl. WS10: Darl 1H 25
WS10: W'bry 5H 25
Boswell Rd. WV14: Bils 5E 19
Boundary Cl. WV13: W'hall 3B 18
Boundary Ind. Est.
WV10: F'hses 3D 4
Boundary Way WV4: Penn 1F 21
WV6: Tett 2C 14
Bourne Av. DY4: Tip 6H 25
Bourne St. WV14: Cose 6H 23
Bowdler Rd.
WV2: Wolv 4E 17 (6D 26)
Bowen Av. WV4: E'shll 3H 23
Bowen-Cooke Av. WV6: Pert 4B 8
Bowen St. WV4: E'shll 1F 23
Bowker St. WV13: W'hall 3B 18
Bowmans Ri. WV1: Wolv 1H 17
Bowness Gro. WV12: W'hall 1G 13
Bowood Dr. WV6: Tett 4G 9
Bow St. WV13: W'hall 3G 19
WV14: Bils 6D 18
Boydon Cl. WV2: E'shll 6H 17
Bracken Cl. WV8: Pend 1H 9
Brackenwood Dr. WV11: Wed 5E 13
Bradburn Rd. WV11: Wed 2A 12
Braden Rd. WV4: Penn 3G 21
Bradgate Cl. WV12: W'hall 4H 13
BRADLEY 3D 24
Bradley La. WV14: Bils 3E 25
Bradley's La. DY4: Tip 6C 24
WV14: Cose 6C 24
Bradley St. WV14: Bils 2E 25
BRADMORE 4H 15
Bradmore Rd. WV3: Wolv 4A 16
Bradshaw Av. WS10: Darl 1G 25
Bradshaw St. WV1: Wolv 2F 17
Braemar Cl. DY3: Sed 5D 22
WV12: W'hall 4G 13
Brailsford Cl. WV11: Wed 2D 12

Church La.—Dover St.

Church La. WV2: Wolv 3D **16** (5A **26**)
WV8: Cod 4C **2**
Church M. DY4: Tip 6E **25**
Church Rd. WV3: Wolv 5H **15**
WV6: Pert 6B **8**
WV6: Tett 5H **9**
(Rock, The)
WV6: Tett 1E **15**
(School Rd.)
WV8: Cod 4C **2**
(not continuous)
WV10: Oxl 1D **10**
WV12: W'hall 4H **13**
WV14: Cose 5C **24**
Church St. WS10: Darl 5H **19**
(Bell St.)
WS10: Darl 2G **25**
(Black Country New Rd.)
WV2: Wolv 3D **16** (5A **26**)
WV10: Wolv 6H **11**
WV11: Wed 5B **12**
WV13: W'hall 2G **19**
(not continuous)
WV14: Bils 1C **24**
Church Wlk. WV3: Wolv 5A **16**
WV6: Tett 5H **9**
WV13: W'hall 3G **19**
Churchward Gro. WV5: Wom 6D **20**
Churnet Gro. WV6: Pert 6C **8**
CINDER HILL **5G 23**
Cineworld Cinema
Wednesfield **6A 12**
Circuit Cl. WV13: W'hall 1G **19**
Clanfield Av. WV11: Wed 2E **13**
Clapgate Gdns. WV14: Cose 3H **23**
Clare Av. WV11: Wed 1E **13**
Clare Cres. WV14: Cose 4G **23**
Claremont M. WV3: Wolv 5B **16**
Claremont Rd. DY3: Sed 6F **23**
WV3: Wolv 5B **16**
Claremont St. WV14: Bils 6B **18**
Clarence Rd.
WV1: Wolv 2D **16** (2A **26**)
WV14: Bils 5D **18**
Clarence St.
WV1: Wolv 2D **16** (3A **26**)
Clarendon Dr. DY4: Tip 5H **25**
Clarendon St. WV3: Wolv 2B **16**
Clare Rd. WV10: Bush 3F **11**
Clarke's La. WV13: W'hall 1H **19**
Clark Rd. WV3: Wolv 2A **16**
Claverley Dr. WV4: Penn 1G **21**
Clayton Cl. WV2: Wolv 5D **16**
Clee Hill Dr. WV3: Wolv 3D **14**
Clee Vw. Mdw. DY3: Sed 4E **23**
Clematis Dr. WV9: Pend 5A **4**
Clem Attlee Ct. WV14: Wolv 4B **18**
Clement Pl. WV14: Bils 5C **18**
Clement Rd. WV14: Bils 5C **18**
Clemson St. WV13: W'hall 2F **19**
Cleveland Cl. WV11: Wed 1E **13**
WV13: W'hall 3C **18**
Cleveland Pas.
WV1: Wolv 3D **16** (4B **26**)
Cleveland Rd.
WV2: Wolv 3E **17** (5D **26**)
Cleveland St.
WV1: Wolv 3D **16** (4B **26**)
Clewley Dr. WV9: Pend 5B **4**
Clifford St. WV6: Wolv 1B **16**
Clift Cl. WV12: W'hall 4H **13**
Clifton Gdns. WV8: Bilb 5F **3**
Clifton Rd. WV6: Tett 5G **9**
Clifton St. WV14: Cose 5G **23**
Clinton Rd. WV14: Bils 5F **19**
Clothier Gdns. WV13: W'hall 1F **19**
Clothier St. WV13: W'hall 1F **19**
Cloverdale WV6: Pert 6A **8**
Clover Ley WV10: Wolv 1G **17**
Club La. WV10: Cov H 2D **4**
Coalport Rd. WV1: Wolv 3H **17**
Coalway Av. WV3: Penn 6B **16**
Coalway Gdns. WV3: Wolv 6G **15**
Coalway Rd. WV3: Penn 6G **15**
Coatsgate Wlk. WV8: Pend 1A **10**
Cobden Cl. DY4: Tip 6E **25**
Cockshutt La. WV2: Wolv 5E **17**
Cocton Cl. WV6: Pert 5B **8**
CODSALL 4C **2**
Codsall Gdns. WV8: Cod 4B **2**
Codsall Ho. WV8: Cod 4B **2**
Codsall Leisure Cen. **4D 2**
Codsall Rd. WV6: Tett 3H **9**
WV8: Tett 1F **9**
Codsall Station (Rail) **5B 2**
Codsall Wood Rd.
WV8: Cod, Cod W 3A **2**
Colaton Cl. WV10: Wolv 6F **11**
Coldridge Cl. WV8: Pend 1A **10**
Coleman St. WV6: Wolv 6A **10**
Coleridge Dr. WV6: Pert 6B **8**
Colesden Wlk. WV4: Penn 6F **15**
College Ct. WV6: Tett 6G **9**
College Rd. WV6: Tett 6G **9**
College Vw. WV6: Tett 1G **15**
Collett Rd. WV6: Pert 5B **8**
Colley Av. WV10: Bush 2G **11**
Collier's Cl. WV12: W'hall 4G **13**
Colliery Rd. WV1: Wolv 2G **17**
Collingwood Rd. WV10: Bush 6F **5**
Colman Av. WV11: Wed 4E **13**
Coltham Rd. WV12: W'hall 4H **13**
COLTON HILLS 2B **22**
Colton Hills Sports Cen. **2C 22**
Coltsfoot Cl. WV11: Wed 5D **12**
Colville Cl. DY4: Tip 6H **25**
Commercial Rd. WV1: Wolv 3F **17**
COMPTON 2F **15**
Compton Ct. WV3: Wolv 2A **16**
Compton Hill Dr. WV3: Wolv 2G **15**
COMPTON HOSPICE **2F 15**
Compton Pk. WV3: Wolv 2H **15**
Compton Pk. Recreation Cen. **1H 15**
Compton Rd. WV3: Wolv 2H **15**
Compton Rd. W. WV3: Wolv 2F **15**
Coniston Rd. WV6: Tett 2G **9**
Connaught Dr. WV5: Wom 5D **20**
Connaught Ho. WV1: Wolv 2B **16**
Connaught Rd. WV1: Wolv 2B **16**
WV14: Bils 5E **19**
Consort Dr. WS10: Darl 4H **19**
Constantine Way WV14: Bils 4F **25**
Convent Cl. WV2: Wolv 3E **17** (5C **26**)
Conway Cres. WV12: W'hall 3H **13**
Conway Rd. WV6: Pert 1C **14**
Cook Cl. WV6: Pert 6B **8**
WV10: Oxl 1D **10**
Cook St. WV2: Wolv 5D **16**
Coombe Cft. WV9: Pend 5B **4**
Cooper St. WV2: Wolv 4G **17**
Copes Cres. WV10: Wolv 4H **11**
Coppice, The DY4: Tip 5H **25**
WV12: W'hall 4H **13**
Coppice Cl. DY3: Sed 6C **22**
WV11: Wed 1F **13**
Coppice Farm Way
WV12: W'hall 1G **13**
Coppice La. WV6: Tett 4E **9**
WV12: W'hall 4H **13**
Coppice Rd. WV3: Wolv 4G **15**
WV14: Cose 6H **23**
Copthorne Rd. WV3: Wolv 5B **16**
Corfe Cl. WV6: Pert 1C **14**
Corfe Rd. WV14: Cose 6H **23**
Corfton Dr. WV6: Tett 6F **9**
Cornfield WV8: Pend 1H **9**
Cornflower Cl. WV10: F'stne 1H **5**
Corn Hill WV10: Wolv 2E **17** (3D **26**)
Cornmill Gro. WV6: Pert 1A **14**
Cornovian Cl. WV6: Pert 5B **8**
Cornwall Ga. WV12: W'hall 5G **13**
Cornwall Rd. WV6: Tett 6F **9**
Coronation Rd. DY4: Tip 6F **25**
WV10: Wolv 5H **11**
WV14: Bils 1B **24**
Corporation St.
WV1: Wolv 2D **16** (3A **26**)
Corsers Ct. WV6: Pert 6B **8**
Corser St. WV1: Wolv 3G **17**
Corve Gdns. WV6: Tett 5H **9**
Corve Vw. DY3: Sed 5D **22**
COSELEY 6B **24**
Coseley Baths **5C 24**
Coseley Hall WV14: Cose 6B **24**
Coseley Leisure Cen. **5A 24**
Coseley Rd. WV14: Bils 1B **24**
Coseley Station (Rail) **5B 24**
Cosford Ct. WV6: Pert 5B **8**
Cosgrove Wlk. WV8: Pend 1A **10**
Coton Rd. WV4: Penn 1C **22**
Cotsdale Rd. WV4: Penn 3H **21**
Cotswold Gro. WV12: W'hall 1G **13**
Cotswold Rd. WV2: E'shll 5G **17**
Cotsworld Ct. *WV2: Wolv 6C **16***
(off Goldthorn Hill)
Cottage Cl. WV11: Wed 4B **12**
(not continuous)
Cottage La. WV10: F'hses 5E **5**
Cottage Vw. WV8: Bilb 4E **3**
Cotwall End Rd.
DY3: Lwr G, Sed 6D **22**
Coulter Gro. WV6: Pert 6A **8**
Council Cres. WV12: W'hall 6H **13**
Courtlands, The WV6: Wolv 6H **9**
Court Rd. WV4: E'shll 3H **23**
WV6: Wolv 6A **10**
COVEN HEATH 2E **5**
Coven La. WV9: Coven 3A **4**
COVEN LAWN 1C **4**
Coventry St. WV1: Wolv 2H **17**
Covert, The WV8: Pend 1H **9**
Cox Rd. WV14: Cose 5D **24**
Coxwell Av. WV10: Wolv 4D **10**
Craddock St. WV6: Wolv 6B **10**
Cramp Hill WS10: Darl 6H **19**
Cranbourne Av. WV4: E'shll 3F **23**
Cranbrook Ct. *WV13: W'hall 2H **19***
(off Mill St.)
Cranbrook Gro. WV6: Pert 1C **14**
Crane Rd. WV14: Bils 3E **25**
Cranesbill Cl. WV10: F'stne 1B **6**
Crane Ter. WV6: Tett 5H **9**
Cranford Rd. WV3: Wolv 4F **15**
Cranleigh Cl. WV12: W'hall 1H **13**
Cranley Dr. WV8: Cod 4C **2**
Cranmere Av. WV6: Tett 4D **8**
Cranmere Ct. WV6: Tett 4D **8**
Cranmore Cl. DY4: Tip 6F **25**
Cranmore Rd. WV3: Wolv 1A **16**
Crantock Cl. WV11: Ess 1H **13**
Crathorne Av. WV10: Oxl 1D **10**
Craven St. WV2: E'shll 6G **17**
Crawford Av. WS10: Darl 5H **19**
WV4: E'shll 3G **23**
Crawford Rd. WV3: Wolv 2B **16**
Crescent, The WV6: Tett 1E **15**
WV13: W'hall 3H **19**
WV14: Bils 6C **18**
Crescent, The (MM) **6C 18**
Crescent Rd. WV13: W'hall 2H **19**
Cresswell Ct. WV9: Pend 5B **4**
Crestwood Glen WV6: Tett 3H **9**
Cricket Mdw. WV10: F'hses 4E **5**
Criterion Works WV13: W'hall 4G **19**
Crocus Cres. WV9: Pend 5B **4**
Croft, The DY3: Sed 5F **23**
WV12: W'hall 4H **13**
Croft Apartments *WV13: W'hall 2F **19***
(off Croft St.)
Crofters Wlk. WV8: Pend 1H **9**
Croft Ind. Est. WV13: W'hall 2F **19**
Croft La. WV10: Bush 3H **11**
Croft St. WV13: W'hall 2F **19**
(not continuous)
Cromer Gdns. WV6: Wolv 5A **10**
Crompton Ct. WV8: Bilb 4E **3**
Cromwell Rd. WV10: Bush 5F **5**
Crosby Cl. WV6: Wolv 5A **10**
Cross Ho. *WV2: Wolv 5D **16***
(off Blakenhall Gdns.)
Crossland Cres. WV6: Tett 4A **10**
Cross La. DY3: Sed 6E **23**
Cross Pl. DY3: Sed 5F **23**
Cross St. WS10: Darl 5H **19**
WV1: Wolv 3G **17**
WV13: W'hall 3F **19**
WV14: Bils 4D **24**
(not continuous)
Cross St. Nth. WV1: Wolv 6E **11**
Cross St. Sth. WV2: Wolv 5D **16**
Crossways Shop. Cen.
WV10: Wolv 1H **17**
Crosswell Way WV14: Bils 1D **24**
Crowesbridge M. WV14: Cose 6A **24**
Crowland Av. WV6: Pert 6B **8**
Crown Cl. DY3: Sed 5E **23**
Crown Ct. WS10: Darl 4H **19**
Crown St. WV1: Wolv 6E **11**
Crowther Gro. WV6: Wolv 6A **10**
Crowther Rd. WV6: Wolv 6H **9**
Crowther St. WV10: Wolv 6F **11**
Croxley Gdns. WV13: W'hall 4E **19**
Crucible, The WV14: Cose 4B **24**
Cullwick St. WV1: Wolv 5H **17**
Culwell Ind. Est. WV10: Wolv 1F **17**
Culwell St.
WV10: Wolv 1E **17** (1D **26**)
Culwell Trad. Est.
WV10: Wolv 6G **11**
Cumberland Ho. WV1: Wolv 6D **10**
Cumberland Rd. WV13: W'hall 2H **19**
WV14: Bils 5C **18**
Cunningham Rd. WV6: Pert 6B **8**
Cupfields Av. DY4: Tip 6G **25**
Curtin Dr. WS10: Mox 2G **25**
Curzon St. WV2: Wolv 5E **17**
Cygnet Cl. WV6: Tett 2F **15**
Cyprus St. WV2: Wolv 6D **16**

D

Dace Rd. WV10: Wolv 6A **12**
Dahlia Ct. WV1: Wolv 3B **18**
Daisy St. WV14: Cose 4C **24**
Daisy Wlk. WV9: Pend 5B **4**
Dalbeg Cl. WV8: Pend 2H **9**
Dale End WS10: Darl 6H **19**
(not continuous)
Dales Cl. WV6: Wolv 4C **10**
Dale St. WV3: Wolv 3C **16** (5A **26**)
WV14: Bils 1E **25**
Daley Rd. WV14: Bils 4E **25**
Dalwood Cl. WV14: Cose 6A **24**
Damson Cl. WV12: W'hall 4F **13**
Danehill Wlk. WV8: Pend 2A **10**
Danes Cl. WV11: Ess 4E **7**
Danescourt Rd. WV6: Tett 4F **9**
Dangerfield La. WS10: Darl 1H **25**
Darby Cl. WV14: Cose 4H **23**
Darkhouse La. WV14: Cose 4B **24**
Dark La. WV10: C Grn 1E **5**
WV10: F'stne, Share 1B **6**
WV10: Share 1B **6**
Darlaston La. WV14: Bils 5F **19**
Darlaston Rd. Ind. Est.
WS10: Darl 1H **25**
Darley Dr. WV6: Wolv 5C **10**
Darlington St.
WV1: Wolv 2C **16** (3A **26**)
WV3: Wolv 2C **16**
Dartmouth Av. WV13: W'hall 2F **19**
Dartmouth Cres. WV14: Bils 5F **19**
Dartmouth St.
WV2: Wolv 4E **17** (6D **26**)
(not continuous)
Darwin Ct. WV6: Pert 6B **8**
Davena Gro. WV14: Cose 3C **24**
Davenport Rd. WV6: Tett 5E **9**
WV11: Wed 4D **12**
Davies Av. WV14: Cose 3C **24**
Davis Rd. WV12: W'hall 2H **13**
Dawn Dr. DY4: Tip 4H **25**
Dawson Av. WV14: Cose 4H **23**
Dawson Sq. WV14: Bils 1B **24**
Day Av. WV11: Wed 3D **12**
Day Ho. DY4: Tip 6H **25**
Dean Ct. WV6: Pert 4B **8**
Deanery Row
WV1: Wolv 1D **16** (1B **26**)
Deansfield Rd. WV1: Wolv 2H **17**
Dean's Rd. WV1: Wolv 1H **17**
Dean St. DY3: Sed 6E **23**
Deborah Cl. WV2: Penn 6D **16**
DEEPFIELDS **4A 24**
Deer Wlk. WV8: Pend 6A **4**
Delamere Rd. WV12: W'hall 3H **13**
Delhurst Rd. WV4: E'shll 3F **23**
Dene Rd. WV4: Lwr P 2C **20**
Denham Gdns. WV3: Wolv 4E **15**
Denise Dr. WV14: Cose 6A **24**
Denmark Cl. WV6: Wolv 6B **10**
Denmead Dr. WV11: Wed 2E **13**
Denmore Gdns. WV1: Wolv 2A **18**
Denstone Gdns. WV10: Bush 5F **5**
Denville Cl. WV14: Bils 5D **18**
Derby Av. WV6: Tett 3H **9**
Dereham Wlk. WV14: Bils 4D **24**
Derry St. WV2: Wolv 4E **17**
Derwent Cl. WV13: W'hall 2H **19**
Derwent Rd. WV6: Tett 2G **9**
Devil's Elbow La.
WV11: Wed 3D **12**
Devon Rd. WV1: Wolv 1C **16**
Devoran Cl. WV6: Wolv 6C **10**
Dewsbury Dr. WV4: Penn 3B **22**
Deyncourt Rd. WV10: Wolv 3H **11**
Diane Cl. DY4: Tip 4G **25**
Dibble Cl. WV12: W'hall 5H **13**
Dickens Rd. WV10: Bush 2H **11**
WV14: Cose 4C **24**
Dickinson Av. WV10: Bush 2F **11**
Dick Sheppard Av. DY4: Tip 6G **25**
Dilloway's La. WV13: W'hall 3D **18**
Dimmingsdale Rd.
WV4: Lwr P 1B **20**
Dimminsdale WV13: W'hall 3F **19**
Dimmocks Av. WV14: Cose 6C **24**
Dimmock St. WV4: E'shll 1F **23**
Dingle, The WV3: Wolv 3G **15**
Dingle La. WV13: W'hall 6F **13**
Dinsdale Wlk. WV6: Wolv 5B **10**
Dippons Dr. WV6: Tett 1D **14**
Dippons La. WV6: Pert 4B **8**
WV6: Tett 4C **8**
Dippons Mill Cl. WV6: Tett 1D **14**
Dirtyfoot La. WV4: Lwr P 1D **20**
Dixon St. WV2: E'shll 6F **17**
Dobbs St. WV2: Wolv 4D **16** (6B **26**)
Dock Mdw. Dr. WV4: E'shll 2H **23**
Doctor's Piece WV13: W'hall 2G **19**
Doe Bank Rd. DY4: Tip 5H **25**
Dooley Cl. WV13: W'hall 2D **18**
Dorchester Cl. WV12: W'hall 2H **13**
Dorchester Rd. WV12: W'hall 2H **13**
Dormston Dr. DY3: Sed 6F **23**
Dormston Sports & Art Cen. **6F 23**
Dorsett Rd. WS10: Darl 6H **19**
Dorsett Rd. Ter. WS10: Darl 6H **19**
Douglas Davies Cl.
WV12: W'hall 6H **13**
Douglas Pl. WV10: Oxl 4D **10**
Douglas Rd. WV14: Cose 6C **24**
Dovecote Cl. WV6: Tett 6F **9**
Dovedale Av. WV12: W'hall 5F **13**
Dovedale Ct. WV4: E'shll 4G **23**
Dovedale Rd. WV4: E'shll 3F **23**
Dover St. WV14: Bils 6C **18**

Downend Cl.—Gandy Rd.

Downend Cl. WV10: Bush 4G **5**
Downham Pl. WV3: Wolv 4A **16**
Downie Rd. WV8: Bilb 5F **3**
Downing Cl. WV11: Wed 3F **13**
Downs, The WV10: Oxl 4D **10**
Downs Rd. WV13: W'hall 4H **19**
Dowty Way WV9: Pend 5B **4**
Drakes Grn. WV14: Bils 3E **25**
Drancy Av. WV12: W'hall 4H **13**
(not continuous)
Draycott Cl. WV4: Penn 1F **21**
Drayton St. WV2: Wolv 4D **16**
Dresden Cl. WV4: E'shll 2H **23**
Drive, The WV6: Tett 5F **9**
WV8: Cod 5C **2**
Drive Flds. WV4: Lwr P 6E **15**
Droveway, The WV8: Pend 6H **3**
WV9: Pend 6H **3**
Droxford Wlk. WV8: Pend 1H **9**
Druid Pk. Rd. WV12: W'hall 1H **13**
Drummond Cl. WV11: Wed 6F **7**
Drummond St.
WV1: Wolv 1D **16** (1A **26**)
Drury La. WV8: Cod 4C **2**
Dryden Cl. DY4: Tip 6F **25**
Dryden Rd. WV10: Bush 1G **11**
Duckhouse Rd. WV11: Wed 3C **12**
Duck La. WV8: Bilb 6E **3**
WV14: Bils 1D **24**
Dudding Rd. WV4: Penn 1E **23**
Dudley Cres. WV11: Wed 4D **12**
Dudley Rd. WV2: Wolv . . .4E **17** (6C **26**)
Dudley St. DY3: Sed 6E **23**
WV1: Wolv 2D **16** (3B **26**)
WV14: Bils 1C **24**
Dudley Wlk. WV4: Penn 1D **22**
Duffield Cl. WV8: Pend 1A **10**
Duke St. WV1: Wolv 3F **17**
WV3: Wolv 5B **16**
WV11: Wed 5C **12**
Dumbleberry Av. DY3: Sed 6D **22**
Dunkley St. WV1: Wolv . . .1D **16** (1A **26**)
Dunlin Dr. WV10: F'stne 1H **5**
Dunsfold Cl. WV14: Cose 3H **23**
Dunsley Gro. WV4: Penn 2B **22**
Dunstall Av. WV6: Wolv 5D **10**
DUNSTALL HILL **5C 10**
Dunstall Hill WV6: Wolv 5D **10**
Dunstall Hill Trad. Est.
WV6: Wolv 5D **10**
Dunstall La. WV6: Wolv 5B **10**
Dunstall Pk. **4B 10**
Dunstall Pk. WV6: Wolv 4C **10**
Dunstall Rd. WV6: Wolv 6C **10**
Dunster Gro. WV6: Pert 1C **14**
D'Urberville Cl. *WV2: E'shll 6G 17*
(off D'urberville Rd.)
D'Urberville Rd. WV2: E'shll 5G **17**
(not continuous)
Durberville Rd. Ind. Est.
WV2: E'shll 5G **17**
Durham Av. WV13: W'hall 1H **19**
Durham Ho. WV1: Wolv 6D **10**
Dursley Cl. WV12: W'hall 6H **13**

E

Eachus Rd. WV14: Cose 6C **24**
Eagle Ct. WV3: Wolv 6B **16**
Eagle St. WV2: Wolv 4F **17**
WV3: Wolv 5B **16**
Earl St. WV14: Bils 1C **24**
WV14: Cose 6C **24**
Earlswood Cres. WV9: Pend 5B **4**
Eastacre WV13: W'hall 3F **19**
East Av. WV11: Wed 4B **12**
Eastcote Rd. WV10: Wolv 5G **11**
E. Croft Rd. WV4: Penn 2F **21**
Eastern Cl. WS10: Mox 3H **25**
Eastfield Gro. WV1: Wolv 2G **17**
Eastfield Retreat WV1: Wolv 2G **17**
Eastfield Rd. DY4: Tip 6F **25**
WV1: Wolv 2G **17**
East Grn. WV4: Penn 6G **15**
Eastleigh DY3: Sed 6D **22**
Eastney Cres. WV8: Pend 2H **9**
Easton Gdns. WV11: Wed 5E **13**
E. Park Trad. Est. WV1: Wolv 4G **17**
East Pk. Way WV1: Wolv 3A **18**
East Rd. DY4: Tip 6G **25**
WV10: B'frd, F'stne 1H **5**
East St. WV1: Wolv 3F **17**
Eastward Glen WV8: Bilb 1F **9**
Eaton Ri. WV12: W'hall 4G **13**
Eaves Ct. Dr. DY3: Sed 5D **22**
Ebenezer St. WV14: Cose 6A **24**
EBSTREE 2A **20**
Ebstree Rd. WV5: Seis, Try 2A **20**
Eccleshall Av. WV10: Oxl 2C **10**
Ecclestone Rd. WV11: Wed 2F **13**
Echo Way WV4: E'shll 2H **23**
Edale Cl. WV4: E'shll 3F **23**
Eden Gdns. DY3: Sed 6F **23**
Edensor Cl. WV10: Wolv 6F **11**
Edge Hill Av. WV10: Bush 6H **5**
Edge Hill Dr. DY3: Sed 4D **22**
WV6: Pert 1B **14**
Edge St. WV14: Cose 6C **24**
Edgeworth Cl. WV12: W'hall 6H **13**
Edinburgh Dr. WV12: W'hall 4G **13**
Edinburgh Rd. WV14: Bils 3E **25**
Edmoor Cl. WV12: W'hall 4H **13**
Ednam Gro. WV5: Wom 5D **20**
Ednam Rd. WV4: Penn 6D **16**
Edward Cl. WV14: Bils 3D **24**
Edward Rd. WV6: Pert 5B **8**
Edward St. WV4: E'shll 6G **17**
Egelwin Cl. WV6: Pert 5B **8**
Egerton Rd. WV10: Bush 5F **5**
Egmont Gdns. WV11: Wed 4E **13**
Elan Rd. DY3: Sed 6D **22**
Eldon St. WS10: Darl 5H **19**
Eldridge Cl. WV9: Pend 6A **4**
Eleanor Rd. WV14: Bils 6C **18**
Elford Gro. WV14: Bils 2B **24**
Elgin Cl. DY3: Sed 5F **23**
Elgin Ct. WV6: Pert 6B **8**
Eliot Cft. WV14: Cose 4C **24**
Elizabeth Av. WV4: Penn 1C **22**
WV14: Bils 3E **25**
Elizabeth Wlk. DY4: Tip 5F **25**
Ellards Dr. WV11: Wed 5E **13**
Ellenvale Cl. WV14: Cose 6H **23**
Ellerton Wlk. WV10: Wolv 5G **11**
Elliotts La. WV8: Cod 5D **2**
Elm Av. WV11: Wed 2A **12**
WV14: Bils 6C **18**
Elmcroft Gdns. WV10: Bush 5F **5**
Elmdale Rd. WV4: Penn 1B **22**
WV14: Cose 6H **23**
Elmdon Cl. WV10: Oxl 1B **10**
Elmdon Rd. WV10: Oxl 1B **10**
Elm Farm Rd. WV2: Wolv 5E **17**
Elm Gro. WV8: Bilb 5D **2**
Elmley Gro. WV6: Pert 1C **14**
Elmsdale WV6: Tett 2D **14**
Elm St. WV3: Wolv 3B **16**
WV13: W'hall 2H **19**
Elmwood Av. WV11: Ess 5F **7**
Elmwood Ri. DY3: Sed 5C **22**
Elston Hall La. WV10: Bush 1E **11**
Elton Cl. WV10: Bush 4F **5**
Elviron Dr. WV6: Tett 5E **9**
Elwells Cl. WV14: Cose 3H **23**
Emerson Gro. WV10: Bush 2G **11**
Emerson Rd. WV10: Bush 1G **11**
Empress Way WS10: Darl 4H **19**
Emsworth Cres. WV9: Pend 6B **4**
Enderby Dr. WV4: Penn 2A **22**
End Hall Rd. WV6: Tett 1D **14**
Engine La. WS10: Mox 2F **25**
Ennerdale Dr. WV6: Pert 6C **8**
Ennerdale Rd. WV6: Tett 2G **9**
Ensbury Cl. WV12: W'hall 6H **13**
Ensdale Row WV13: W'hall 3F **19**
Enville Rd. WV4: Penn 2F **21**
Epsom Cl. WV6: Pert 6C **8**
Ermington Rd. WV4: Penn 1E **23**
Ernest Clarke Cl.
WV12: W'hall 6H **13**
Eskdale Cl. WV1: Wolv 2H **17**
Esporta Health Club
Broadlands **3E 5**
Essex Ho. WV1: Wolv 6D **10**
ESSINGTON **5F 7**
Essington Ind. Est. WV11: Ess 4E **7**
Essington Rd. WV12: W'hall 6G **7**
Essington Way WV1: Wolv 3A **18**
Etheridge Rd. WV14: Bils 5B **18**
Etruria Way WV14: Bils 5D **18**
ETTINGSHALL **1H 23**
ETTINGSHALL PARK **2F 23**
Ettingshall Pk. Farm La.
WV4: E'shll 2F **23**
Ettingshall Rd. WV2: E'shll 5H **17**
WV14: Cose 4H **23**
Ettymore Cl. DY3: Sed 6E **23**
Ettymore Rd. DY3: Sed 6E **23**
Ettymore Rd. W. DY3: Sed 6D **22**
Evans Pl. WV14: Bils 5D **18**
Evans St. WV6: Wolv 6B **10**
WV13: W'hall 3C **18**
WV14: Cose 5G **23**
Evenlode Gro. WV13: W'hall 3H **19**
Evergreen Cl. WV14: Cose 6A **24**
Eversley Gro. DY3: Sed 4D **22**
WV11: Wed 4B **12**
Ewhurst Cl. WV13: W'hall 4E **19**
Exbury Cl. WV9: Pend 6A **4**
Exchange St.
WV1: Wolv 2D **16** (3B **26**)
Exmoor Grn. WV11: Wed 3B **12**
Exton Cl. WV11: Wed 2E **13**
Eyston Av. DY4: Tip 6H **25**
Ezekiel La. WV12: W'hall 4H **13**

F

Factory St. WS10: Darl 6H **19**
Fairfax Rd. WV10: Bush 6E **5**
Fairfield Dr. WV8: Cod 4B **2**
Fairhills DY3: Sed 6E **23**
Fairlawn Cl. WV12: W'hall 1H **13**
Fairlawn Way WV12: W'hall 1H **13**
Fairoak Dr. WV6: Tett 1E **15**
Fairview Cl. WV11: Wed 4A **12**
Fairview Cres. WV11: Wed 3A **12**
Fairview Gro. WV11: Wed 3A **12**
Fairview Rd. WV4: Penn 2F **21**
WV11: Wed 3A **12**
Fairway Grn. WV14: Bils 5C **18**
Falcon Cres. WV14: Cose 4G **23**
Falcondale Rd. WV12: W'hall 1H **13**
FALLINGS PARK **5G 11**
Fallings Pk. Ind. Est.
WV10: Wolv 5G **11**
Fallowfield WV6: Pert 6A **8**
WV8: Pend 6H **3**
Fancourt Av. WV4: Penn 2G **21**
Fane Rd. WV11: Wed 1F **13**
Farbrook Way WV12: W'hall 4G **13**
Fareham Cres. WV4: Penn 6F **15**
Farleigh Dr. WV3: Wolv 4D **14**
Farleigh Rd. WV6: Pert 1D **14**
Farmbridge Cl. WS2: Wals 1H **19**
Farmbridge Way WS2: Wals 1H **19**
Farmbrook Av. WV10: F'hses 5E **5**
Farm Cl. WV8: Bilb 6E **3**
Farmers Fold
WV1: Wolv 2D **16** (3B **26**)
Farmer Way DY4: Tip 5G **25**
Farmoor Way WV10: Bush 4F **5**
Farm Rd. WV3: Wolv 4F **15**
Farmside Grn. WV9: Pend 6A **4**
Farndale Av. WV6: Wolv 5A **10**
Farrington Rd. WV4: E'shll 3E **23**
Farway Gdns. WV8: Cod 6C **2**
Faulkland Cres.
WV1: Wolv 1E **17** (1C **26**)
Faversham Cl. WV8: Pend 2H **9**
Fawdry St. WV1: Wolv 1C **16**
Fawley Cl. WV13: W'hall 4E **19**
FEATHERSTONE **1A 6**
Fellows Rd. WV14: Bils 5C **18**
Fellows St. WV2: Wolv 4D **16**
Fenmere Cl. WV4: Penn 1E **23**
Fenn Ri. WV12: W'hall 4G **13**
Fereday's Cft. DY3: Sed 6E **23**
Fereday St. DY4: Tip 6E **25**
Ferguson St. WV11: Wed 1F **13**
Fern Cl. WV14: Cose 6A **24**
Ferndale Rd. WV11: Ess 5G **7**
Ferndown Gdns. WV11: Wed 5E **13**
Fern Leys WV3: Wolv 3G **15**
Fern Rd. WV3: Wolv 4C **16**
Fernside Rd. WV13: W'hall 1C **18**
Festival Av. WS10: Darl 2H **25**
Festival Way WV6: Wolv 5C **10**
Fibbersley WV11: Wed 6E **13**
WV13: W'hall 6E **13**
Fibbersley Bank
WV13: W'hall 6E **13**
Fld. Head Pl. WV6: Tett 6E **9**
Fieldhouse Rd. WV4: E'shll 2F **23**
Field Rd. DY4: Tip 6E **25**
Fields, The WV8: Bilb 4E **3**
Fieldside Wlk. WV14: Bils 4C **18**
Field St. WV10: Wolv 1F **17**
WV13: W'hall 2F **19**
WV14: Bils 3D **24**
Fieldview Cl. WV14: Cose 4D **24**
Fifth Av. WV10: Bush 3E **11**
Filey Rd. WV10: Oxl 6C **4**
Fincham Cl. WV9: Pend 5B **4**
Finchdene Gro. WV3: Wolv 3G **15**
Finchfield Gdns. WV3: Wolv 3H **15**
Finchfield Hill WV3: Wolv 2F **15**
(not continuous)
Finchfield La. WV3: Wolv 4F **15**
Finchfield Rd. WV3: Wolv 3H **15**
Finchfield Rd. W.
WV3: Wolv 3G **15**
Finneywell Cl. WV14: Cose 3A **24**
Fircroft WV14: Bils 3F **25**
Fir Gro. WV3: Wolv 3B **16**
Firsbrook Cl. WV6: Wolv 5A **10**
Firsbrook Ho. WV6: Wolv 5B **10**
First Av. WV10: Bush 4F **11**
Fir St. DY3: Sed 6A **22**
Firsvale Rd. WV11: Wed 5E **13**
Firsway WV6: Tett 2D **14**
Fir Tree Rd. WV3: Wolv 4G **15**
Fisher St. WV13: W'hall 2H **19**
Fistral Gdns. WV3: Wolv 5A **16**
Fitness First Health Club
Wolverhampton *6C 26*
(in AMF Bowling Express)
Fitzmaurice Rd. WV11: Wed 3E **13**
Five Flds. Rd. WV12: W'hall 5F **13**
Five Oaks Rd. WV13: W'hall 4D **18**
Five Ways WV1: Wolv 6D **10**
WV3: Penn 5F **15**
Flash La. WV4: Lwr P 4B **20**
Flavell Av. WV14: Cose 5C **24**
Flaxton Wlk. WV6: Wolv 5B **10**
Fleet St. WV14: Bils 1C **24**
Flemmynge Cl. WV8: Cod 4B **2**
Fletcher's La. WV13: W'hall 2H **19**
Flint Ho. WV1: Wolv 6D **10**
Florence Av. WV4: E'shll 2G **23**
Florence Rd. WV8: Bilb 5F **3**
Flowerdale Cl. WV14: Cose 6A **24**
Fold, The WS10: Darl 6H **19**
WV4: Penn 2A **22**
WV8: Oaken 6A **2**
Fold St. WV1: Wolv 3D **16** (4A **26**)
Foley Av. WV6: Tett 1F **15**
Foley Dr. WV6: Tett 1F **15**
Fontwell Rd. WV10: F'hses 4E **5**
Fordham Gro. WV9: Pend 5B **4**
Fordhouse Rd. WV10: Bush 1E **11**
Fordhouse Rd. Ind. Est.
WV10: Bush 2E **11**
FORDHOUSES **5C 4**
Forest Ct. WV12: W'hall 2H **13**
Forest Ga. WV12: W'hall 2H **13**
Forge Cl. WV8: Pend 1H **9**
Forge Rd. WS10: Darl 6H **19**
WV12: W'hall 6H **13**
Forge St. WV13: W'hall 1G **19**
Formby Av. WV6: Pert 6A **8**
Forrest Av. WV11: Ess 4F **7**
Forsythia Gro. WV8: Bilb 5D **2**
Forton Cl. WV6: Tett 2E **15**
Foster Av. WV14: Cose 5A **24**
Foster Grn. WV6: Pert 1B **14**
Foster Rd. WV10: Bush 4F **11**
Foster St. WS10: Darl 5H **19**
Foundry St. DY4: Tip 6D **24**
WV14: Bils 2F **25**
WV14: Cose 5B **24**
Fountain La. DY4: Tip 6C **24**
WV14: Cose 6C **24**
Fourth Av. WV10: Bush 4E **11**
Fowler Cl. WV6: Pert 4B **8**
Fowler St. WV2: Wolv 6D **16**
Foxglove Cl. WV10: F'stne 1A **6**
WV11: Wed 5D **12**
Foxhills Rd. WV4: Penn 3F **21**
Fox Hollow WV6: Tett 2F **15**
Foxlands Av. WV4: Penn 3G **21**
Foxlands Cres. WV4: Penn 3F **21**
Foxlands Dr. WV4: Penn 3F **21**
Fox's La. WV1: Wolv 6D **10**
Fozdar Cres. WV14: Cose 5A **24**
Framlingham Gro. WV6: Pert 1D **14**
Francis St. WV1: Wolv 6D **10**
Franklyn Cl. WV6: Pert 5B **8**
Fraser St. WV14: Bils 1D **24**
(not continuous)
Frederick Rd. WV11: Wed 5B **12**
Frederick St.
WV2: Wolv 4D **16** (6B **26**)
Frederick William St.
WV13: W'hall 2G **19**
Freeman Pl. WV14: Bils 4D **18**
Freeman St. WV10: Wolv 2G **17**
Freezeland St. WV14: Bils 6A **18**
Friesland Dr. WV1: Wolv 1A **18**
Froggatt Rd. WV14: Bils 5C **18**
Frome Dr. WV11: Wed 5B **12**
Frost St. WV2: E'shll 6H **17**
Froyle Cl. WV6: Tett 5F **9**
Froysell St. WV13: W'hall 2G **19**
Fryer St. WV1: Wolv 2E **17** (2C **26**)
Fuchsia Dr. WV9: Pend 5A **4**
Fullerton Cl. WV8: Pend 1H **9**
Fullwoods End WV14: Cose 5B **24**
Furlongs, The WV11: Wed 5A **12**

G

Gadsby Av. WV11: Wed 3F **13**
Gail Pk. WV3: Wolv 5G **15**
Gainford Cl. WV8: Pend 1A **10**
Gainsborough Dr. WV6: Pert 6C **8**
Gairloch Rd. WV12: W'hall 1G **13**
Gala Bingo Club
Bushbury **2E 11**
Wednesfield **3E 13**
Galbraith Cl. WV14: Cose 6C **24**
Gallery, The
WV1: Wolv 3D **16** (4B **26**)
Gamesfield Grn. WV3: Wolv 3A **16**
Gandy Rd. WV12: W'hall 4F **13**

A-Z Wolverhampton 31

Lawley Rd.—Middle Cross

Lawley Rd. WV14: Bils 6A **18**
Lawn La. WV9: Coven 3A **4**
Lawn Rd. WV2: E'shll 6G **17**
Lawnside Grn. WV14: Bils 4C **18**
Lawnswood Av. WV4: E'shll 2F **23**
WV6: Tett 2H **9**
Lawnswood Ri. WV6: Tett 2A **10**
Lawrence Av. WV10: Wolv 6H **11**
WV11: Wed 4E **13**
Lawrence St. WV13: W'hall 1F **19**
Lea Av. WS10: W'bry 5H **25**
Lea Bank WV3: Wolv 2F **15**
Leabrook Rd. DY4: Tip 5H **25**
WS10: W'bry 5H **25**
Leacote Dr. WV6: Tett 6F **9**
Leacroft WV12: W'hall 3H **13**
Leacroft Av. WV10: Bush 2F **11**
Lea Gdns. WV3: Wolv 4C **16**
Lea Mnr. Dr. WV4: Penn 3H **21**
Lea Rd. WV3: Wolv 5B **16** (6A **26**)
Lear Rd. WV5: Wom 6E **21**
Leas, The WV10: F'stne 1B **6**
Leason La. WV10: Bush 2H **11**
Leasowe Dr. WV6: Pert 6A **8**
Leasowes Dr. WV4: Penn 6G **15**
Lea Vw. WV12: W'hall 5F **13**
Ledbury Ct. WV12: W'hall 6G **13**
Ledbury Dr. WV1: Wolv 3A **18**
Lees Rd. WV14: Bils 3E **25**
Lees Ter. WV14: Bils 3E **25**
Legge La. WV14: Cose 4C **24**
Legge St. WV2: E'shll 6F **17**
Legs La. WV10: Bush 4F **5**
Leicester Sq. WV6: Wolv 1B **16**
Leicester St. WV6: Wolv 6C **10**
Leighton Rd. WV4: Penn 6A **16**
WV14: Bils 2F **25**
Len Davis Rd. WV12: W'hall 3G **13**
Lennox Gdns. WV3: Wolv 4B **16**
Leslie Dr. DY4: Tip 5F **25**
Leslie Rd. WV10: Wolv 5G **11**
Lesscroft Cl. WV9: Pend 5B **4**
Lester St. WV14: Bils 1E **25**
Leve La. WV13: W'hall 2G **19**
Leven Dr. WV12: W'hall 1G **13**
Lever St. WV2: Wolv 4E **17** (6C **26**)
Leverton Ri. WV10: Oxl 4D **10**
Leveson Ct. WV13: W'hall 2F **19**
Leveson Rd. WV11: Wed 2E **13**
Leveson St. WV13: W'hall 2F **19**
Levington Cl. WV6: Pert 6C **8**
Lewis Av. WV1: Wolv 1A **18**
Lewis Cl. WV12: W'hall 5H **13**
Lewis Gro. WV11: Wed 4C **12**
Lewisham Rd. WV10: Oxl 6C **4**
Lewis St. WV14: Bils 6D **18**
Lewthorn Ri. WV4: Penn 2E **23**
Leybourne Cres. WV9: Pend 6A **4**
Leyland Av. WV3: Wolv 3A **16**
Ley Ri. DY3: Sed 5D **22**
Leys, The WS10: Darl 6H **19**
Lich Av. WV11: Wed 3D **12**
Lichfield Pas.
WV1: Wolv 2E **17** (2C **26**)
Lichfield Rd. WV11: Wed 5C **12**
WV12: W'hall 4D **12**
Lichfield St. DY4: Tip 6E **25**
WV1: Wolv 2D **16** (3B **26**)
WV14: Bils 6C **18**
Lich Gates WV1: Wolv 2D **16** (2B **26**)
Lichwood Rd. WV11: Wed 3E **13**
Lighthouse, The **2E 17** (**2C 26**)
Lilac Rd. WV1: Wolv 4A **18**
Lilian Gro. WV14: Bils 5D **24**
Lilleshall Cres. WV2: Wolv 5E **17**
Lime Gro. WV14: Bils 5B **18**
Limehurst Av. WV3: Wolv 4F **15**
Lime Rd. DY3: Sed 5G **23**
Limes Rd. WV6: Tett 6F **9**
Lime St. WV3: Wolv 4B **16**
WV14: Cose 6H **23**
Lime Tree Av. WV6: Tett 1D **14**
Lime Tree Gdns. WV8: Bilb 5E **3**
Lime Tree Rd. WV8: Bilb 5E **3**
Lincoln Av. WV13: W'hall 1H **19**
Lincoln Grn. WV10: Bush 6E **5**
Lincoln St. WV10: Wolv 1F **17**
Linden Lea WV3: Wolv 3G **15**
Lindens, The WV6: Wolv 1H **15**
Linfield Gdns. DY3: Sed 5D **22**
Lingfield Av. WV10: F'hses 3E **5**
Lingfield Gro. WV6: Pert 6C **8**
Ling Ho. WV10: Wolv 1G **17**
Link Rd. WV5: Wom 6D **20**
Links Av. WV6: Tett 3G **9**
Links Rd. WV4: Penn 3B **22**
Linley Dr. WV10: Bush 1F **11**
Linnet Gro. WV12: W'hall 2G **13**
Linslade Cl. WV4: Penn 2E **23**
Linthouse La. WV11: Wed 2C **12**
Linton Cft. WV14: Bils 1C **24**
Linton Rd. WV4: Penn 1H **21**
Lister St. WV13: W'hall 3G **19**
Little Birches WV3: Wolv 4A **16**
Lit. Brick Kiln St.
WV3: Wolv 3D **16** (5A **26**)
Lit. Clothier St. WV13: W'hall 1F **19**
Lit. Cross St. WS10: Darl 5H **19**
LITTLE LONDON 1F **19**
Lit. Park St.
WV1: Wolv 2E **17** (3D **26**)
Lit. Pountney St.
WV2: Wolv 4D **16** (6B **26**)
Little's La. WV1: Wolv 2E **17** (1C **26**)
(not continuous)
Littleton Rd. WV12: W'hall 3H **13**
Lit. Wood St. WV13: W'hall 2F **19**
Live & Let Live Mobile Home Pk.
WV10: F'stne 1B **6**
Livingstone Av. WV6: Pert 5B **8**
Livingstone Rd. WV14: Bils 1A **24**
Lloyd Dr. WV4: Penn 4F **21**
Lloyd Hill WV4: Penn 3F **21**
Lloyd Rd. WV6: Tett 5G **9**
Lloyd St. WV6: Wolv 6A **10**
Lochalsh Gro. WV12: W'hall 1G **13**
Lockley Cl. WV10: Wolv 6G **11**
Lock Mus. **3F 19**
Locksmith Cl. WV13: W'hall 2G **19**
Lock St. WV1: Wolv 1E **17** (1D **26**)
(not continuous)
Lodge Rd. WS10: Darl 1H **25**
WV10: Oxl 2C **10**
WV14: Bils 2E **25**
Lodge St. WV12: W'hall 5H **13**
Logan Cl. WV10: Oxl 4D **10**
Lomas St. WV1: Wolv 6D **10**
Lomond Rd. DY3: Sed 5D **22**
Long Acre WV8: Cod 6C **2**
Longacre WV13: W'hall 4F **19**
Longdon Av. WV4: Penn 1E **23**
Longfield Ho. WV10: Wolv 1G **17**
Longford Rd. WV10: Wolv 6G **11**
Long Furrow WV8: Pend 1H **9**
Long Knowle La. WV11: Wed 2A **12**
Longlake Av. WV6: Tett 1D **14**
Long La. WS6: Ess, Gt Wyr 3H **7**
Long Ley WV10: Wolv 1G **17**
Long Mdw. Dr. DY3: Sed 4C **22**
Long Mill Av. WV11: Wed 3A **12**
Long Mill Nth. WV11: Wed 3A **12**
Long Mill Sth. WV11: Wed 3A **12**
Longmoor Cl. WV11: Wed 5E **13**
Long Mynd Cl. WV12: W'hall 1G **13**
Long St. WV1: Wolv 2E **17** (2C **26**)
Lonsdale Cl. WV12: W'hall 5G **13**
Lonsdale Rd. WV3: Wolv 5C **16**
WV14: Bils 6E **19**
Lordsmore Cl. WV14: Cose 5D **24**
Lord St. WV3: Wolv 2C **16**
(not continuous)
WV14: Bils 3D **24**
Lord St. W. WV14: Bils 3D **24**
Lorne St. DY4: Tip 6E **25**
Lothians Rd. WV6: Tett 4H **9**
Lovatt Cl. DY4: Tip 5H **25**
Lovatt St. WV1: Wolv 2C **16**
Love La. WV6: Tett 4G **9**
Loveridge Cl. WV8: Cod 5C **2**
Lowbridge Cl. WV12: W'hall 5H **13**
Lowcroft Gdns. WV10: Bush 2F **11**
Lowe Av. WS10: Darl 5G **19**
LOWER BRADLEY 3F **25**
Lower Grn. WV6: Tett 5H **9**
Lwr. Hall St. *WV13: W'hall* *3G* ***19***
(off Walsall St.)
Lwr. Lichfield St. WV13: W'hall 2F **19**
LOWER PENN 1D **20**
Lwr. Prestwood Rd.
WV11: Wed 3B **12**
Lower St. WV6: Tett 5H **9**
Lwr. Vauxhall WV1: Wolv 2B **16**
Lwr. Villiers St. WV2: Wolv 5D **16**
Lowe St. WV6: Wolv 6B **10**
LOW HILL 3F **11**
Low Hill Cres. WV10: Bush 2F **11**
Lowlands Av. WV6: Tett 4H **9**
Lowlands Ct. WV6: Tett 4H **9**
Lowry Cl. WV6: Pert 6C **8**
WV13: W'hall 2D **18**
LOXDALE 2E **25**
Loxdale Ind. Est. WV14: Bils 2D **24**
Loxdale Sidings WV14: Bils 2E **25**
Loxdale St. WV14: Bils 2E **25**
Luce Rd. WV10: Bush 4F **11**
Lucknow Rd. WV12: W'hall 6G **13**
Ludlow Cl. WV12: W'hall 4G **13**
Ludstone Av. WV4: Penn 1G **21**
Lulworth Wlk. WV4: Penn 6F **15**
LUNT, THE 5F **19**
Lunt Pl. WV14: Bils 6F **19**
Lunt Rd. WV14: Bils 6E **19**
Lutley Cl. WV3: Wolv 5H **15**
Lyd Cl. WV11: Wed 5A **12**
Lydham Cl. WV14: Bils 2A **24**
Lydiates Cl. DY3: Sed 6C **22**
Lydney Cl. WV12: W'hall 1H **19**
Lymer Rd. WV10: Oxl 1D **10**
Lymington Rd. WV13: W'hall 2H **19**
Lyndale Dr. WV11: Wed 4D **12**
Lyndale Rd. DY3: Sed 4C **22**
Lyndhurst Rd. WV3: Wolv 5B **16**
Lyndon Cl. DY3: Sed 5F **23**
Lynton Av. WV6: Tett 3H **9**
Lytham Rd. WV6: Pert 6A **8**
Lytton Av. WV4: Penn 2G **21**

M

McBean Rd. WV6: Wolv 6A **10**
McLean Rd. WV10: Oxl 6D **4**
Macrome Rd. WV6: Tett 2H **9**
Madeira Av. WV8: Cod 6D **2**
Magness Cres. WV12: W'hall 5H **13**
Magnolia Gro. WV8: Bilb 5D **2**
WV12: W'hall 6G **13**
Malcolm Ct. WV1: Wolv 1B **16**
Malins Rd. WV4: E'shll 1F **23**
Mallory Rd. WV6: Pert 1B **14**
Mallow Ct. WV6: Wolv 5C **10**
Malpass Gdns. WV8: Cod 4B **2**
Malpas Wlk. WV10: Wolv 5H **11**
Malt Ho. La. WV13: W'hall 2F **19**
Malthouse La. WV6: Tett 4H **9**
Maltings, The
WV1: Wolv 1E **17** (1C **26**)
Malvern Cl. WV12: W'hall 6G **13**
Malvern Ct. WV10: Bush 2E **11**
Malvern Dr. WV1: Wolv 3A **18**
Mammouth Dr. WV10: Wolv 5E **11**
Manby Cl. WV6: Wolv 6C **10**
Manby St. DY4: Tip 6E **25**
Mancroft Gdns. WV6: Tett 5F **9**
Mancroft Rd. WV6: Tett 5F **9**
Mandale Rd. WV10: Wolv 4G **11**
Mander Cen.
WV1: Wolv 2D **16** (3B **26**)
Manderley Cl. DY3: Sed 4D **22**
Manders Ind. Est. WV1: Wolv 1G **17**
Mander Sq. WV1: Wolv 3D **16** (4B **26**)
Mander St. WV3: Wolv 4C **16** (6A **26**)
Manfield Rd. WV13: W'hall 1B **18**
Manlove St. WV3: Wolv 4B **16**
Manor Cl. WV4: Penn 2A **22**
WV8: Bilb 4E **3**
WV13: W'hall 1F **19**
Manor Farm Dr. WV12: W'hall 5H **13**
Manor Fold WV8: Oaken 6A **2**
Manor Ho. Pk. WV8: Bilb 4E **3**
Manor Rd. WV4: E'shll 1H **23**
WV4: Penn 2A **22**
WV10: Oxl 3D **10**
Manor St. WV6: Tett 5F **9**
Mansard Cl. WV3: Wolv 4A **16**
WV11: Bush 2A **12**
Mansell Rd. DY4: Tip 6F **25**
Manston Dr. WV6: Pert 5B **8**
Maple Cen., The WS10: Mox 3G **25**
Maple Dr. WS10: Mox 2G **25**
Maple Gro. WV3: Wolv 2F **15**
WV14: Bils 2E **25**
Maple Leaf Rd. WS10: W'bry 5H **25**
Maple Rd. WV3: Wolv 5H **15**
Marchant Rd. WV3: Wolv 2A **16**
WV14: Bils 5B **18**
MARCH END **5D 12**
March End Rd. WV11: Wed 5C **12**
(not continuous)
Marden Cl. WV13: W'hall 3E **19**
Maree Gro. WV12: W'hall 1G **13**
Margaret Rd. WS10: Darl 2H **25**
Margaret Va. DY4: Tip 5H **25**
Marholm Cl. WV9: Pend 6A **4**
Market La. WV4: Lwr P 6C **14**
Market Pl. WV13: W'hall 3F **19**
Market St. WV1: Wolv 2E **17** (3C **26**)
Market Way WV14: Bils 1C **24**
Markham Cft. WV9: Pend 6B **4**
Marklin Av. WV10: Oxl 1E **11**
Marksbury Cl. WV6: Wolv 5B **10**
Marlborough Gdns. WV6: Wolv 6H **9**
Marlbrook Dr. WV4: Penn 6C **16**
Marlowe Dr. WV12: W'hall 3F **13**
Marnel Dr. WV3: Wolv 4G **15**
Mars Cl. WV14: Cose 5H **23**
Marshall Rd. WV13: W'hall 3B **18**
Marshalls Ind. Est. WV2: Wolv 5D **16**
Marsh La. WV10: F'hses 5C **4**
Marsh La. Pde. WV10: Oxl 6D **4**
Marston Av. WS10: Darl 6H **19**
Marston Rd. WV2: Wolv 5C **16**
Marston Rd. Ind. Est.
WV2: Wolv 5D **16**
Marston St. WV13: W'hall 2H **19**
Martham Dr. WV6: Tett 2E **15**
Martin Cl. WV14: Cose 6C **24**
Martin Dr. WV12: W'hall 5H **13**
Martin Rd. WV14: Bils 3E **25**
Martin St. WV4: E'shll 1G **23**
Mary Ann St. WV1: Wolv 3F **17**
Masefield Cl. WV14: Bils 4E **25**
Masefield M. WV10: Bush 1H **11**
Masefield Rd. WV10: Bush 1H **11**
Maslin Dr. WV14: Cose 5H **23**
Mason Cres. WV4: Penn 1H **21**
Mason St. WV2: Wolv 5D **16**
WV14: Cose 6A **24**
Massbrook Gro. WV10: Wolv 4G **11**
Massbrook Rd. WV10: Wolv 4G **11**
Mattox Rd. WV11: Wed 4C **12**
Maurice Gro. WV10: Wolv 4H **11**
Maxwell Rd.
WV2: Wolv 4E **17** (6D **26**)
Maybury Cl. WV8: Cod 4B **2**
Maybush Gdns. WV10: Oxl 1D **10**
Mayfair Gdns. WV3: Wolv 2G **15**
Mayfield Rd. WV1: Wolv 3A **18**
Mayhurst Cl. DY4: Tip 6F **25**
Mayswood Dr. WV6: Tett 3C **14**
Maythorn Gdns. WV6: Tett 1F **15**
WV8: Bilb 4D **2**
Mead, The DY3: Sed 6C **22**
Meadowbrook Gdns. WV8: Bilb 4E **3**
Meadow Cl. WV12: W'hall 2H **13**
Meadow Cft. WV6: Pert 1A **14**
Mdw. Grange Dr. WV12: W'hall 3H **13**
Meadow La. WV5: Wom 6D **20**
WV10: Cov H 2D **4**
WV12: W'hall 5F **13**
WV14: Cose 4A **24**
(not continuous)
Meadow Rd. WV3: Wolv 4F **15**
Meadow Va. WV8: Bilb 6E **3**
Meadow Vw. DY3: Sed 5D **22**
WV6: Tett 6H **9**
Meadow Vw. Mobile Home Pk.
WV10: Cov H 2D **4**
Meadow Vw. Ter. WV6: Tett 6H **9**
(not continuous)
Meadow Vw. Wharf WV6: Tett 6H **9**
Meadow Way WV8: Cod 6B **2**
Meadway, The WV6: Tett 5D **8**
Meadwood Ind. Est.
WV14: Bils 1D **24**
Measham Way WV11: Wed 3D **12**
Mecca Bingo
Bilston **2B 24**
Wolverhampton **3D 16** (**4A 26**)
Medina Cl. WV10: Bush 4G **5**
Melbourne St.
WV2: Wolv 3E **17** (5C **26**)
Melbury Cl. WV3: Wolv 3B **16**
Meldon Dr. WV14: Bils 4F **25**
Melford Cl. DY3: Sed 4D **22**
Melrose Dr. WV6: Pert 6A **8**
Melverton Av. WV10: Bush 2E **11**
Memorial Cl. WV13: W'hall 2F **19**
Memory La. WS10: Darl 4H **19**
WV11: Wed 5A **12**
Menai Cl. WV12: W'hall 4H **13**
Mendip Cl. WV2: E'shll 6G **17**
Meon Gro. WV6: Pert 6C **8**
Meon Way WV11: Wed 3E **13**
Meranti Cl. WV12: W'hall 2H **13**
Mercer Gro. WV11: Wed 3D **12**
Mercia Dr. WV6: Pert 5B **8**
Mere Cl. WV12: W'hall 5F **13**
Meredith Rd. WV11: Wed 2B **12**
Mere Oak Rd. WV6: Pert 5B **8**
Meriden Rd. WV10: Oxl 2B **10**
Merrick Rd. WV11: Wed 4F **13**
MERRIDALE **3A 16**
Merridale Av. WV3: Wolv 3A **16**
Merridale Ct. WV3: Wolv 3A **16**
Merridale Cres. WV3: Wolv 2B **16**
Merridale Gdns. WV3: Wolv 3B **16**
Merridale Gro. WV3: Wolv 3H **15**
(not continuous)
Merridale La. WV3: Wolv 2B **16**
Merridale Rd. WV3: Wolv 3A **16**
Merridale St.
WV3: Wolv 3C **16** (5A **26**)
Merridale St. W. WV3: Wolv 4B **16**
Merrill's Hall La. WV11: Wed 6D **12**
MERRY HILL
Wolverhampton **5G 15**
Merryhills Ent. Pk.
WV10: Wolv 5G **11**
Merstone Cl. WV14: Bils 6B **18**
Mervyn Pl. WV14: Bils 3E **25**
Mervyn Rd. WV14: Bils 3E **25**
Michael Rd. WS10: Darl 5G **19**
Mickley Av. WV10: Wolv 5F **11**
Midacre WV13: W'hall 3F **19**
Middle Av. WV13: W'hall 4D **18**
Middle Cross
WV1: Wolv 3E **17** (4D **26**)

34 A-Z Wolverhampton

Middlefield—Paget St.

Middlefield WV8: Pend .6H 3
Middle Gdns. WV13: W'hall .2G 19
Middle La. WV8: Oaken .6A 2
WV9: Coven .4A 4
Middleton Trad. Est.
WV13: W'hall .2D 18
Middle Vauxhall WV1: Wolv .2B 16
Middleway Grn. WV14: Bils .4B 18
Middleway Rd. WV14: Bils .4B 18
Midhurst Gro. WV6: Tett .5F 9
Midland Rd. WS10: Darl .4H 19
Milcote Dr. WV13: W'hall .3C 18
Miles Mdw. Cl. WV12: W'hall .2H 13
Milestone Ct. WV6: Tett .1D 14
Milestone Way WV12: W'hall .2G 13
Milford Av. WV12: W'hall .5F 13
Milford Rd. WV2: Wolv .5D 16
Millard Rd. WV14: Cose .5A 24
Mill Bank DY3: Sed .6E 23
Millbank St. WV11: Wed .1E 13
Mill Cft. WV14: Bils .6D 18
Milldale Cres. WV10: F'hses .4E 5
Milldale Rd. WV10: F'hses .4E 5
Millennium Way WV8: Bilb .4E 3
Miller Cres. WV14: Cose .5H 23
Millfields Rd. WV4: E'shll .1H 23
WV14: Bils .1H 23
Mill Grn. WV10: F'hses .4E 5
Mill Gro. WV8: Bilb .5F 3
Millichip Rd. WV13: W'hall .3D 18
Millington Rd. DY4: Tip .5E 25
WV10: Bush .4F 11
Mill La. WV6: Tett .1D 14
WV8: Cod .2B 2
WV11: Wed .3H 11
WV12: W'hall .5H 13
Mills Cl. WV11: Wed .2A 12
Mills Cres. WV2: Wolv .4F 17
Mills Rd. WV2: Wolv .4F 17
Mill Stream Cl. WV8: Bilb .4E 3
Mill St. WS10: Darl .6H 19
WV13: W'hall .2H 19
WV14: Bils .1B 24
Mills Wlk. DY4: Tip .6E 25
Millwalk Dr. WV9: Pend .5B 4
Milton Ct. WV6: Pert .6B 8
Milton Rd. WV10: Wolv .5H 11
WV14: Cose .6C 24
Minehead Rd. WV10: Oxl .6C 4
Minith Rd. WV14: Cose .6C 24
Minster, The WV3: Wolv .5A 16
Minsterley Cl. WV3: Wolv .4H 15
Minton Cl. WV1: Wolv .3H 17
Mirfield Cl. WV9: Pend .5B 4
Mitchell Av. WV14: Cose .5A 24
Mitre Cl. WV11: Ess .5F 7
Mitre Fold WV1: Wolv .2D 16 (2A 26)
Moatbrook Av. WV8: Cod .4B 2
Moatbrook La. WV8: Cod .3A 2
Moat Grn. Av. WV11: Wed .3D 12
Moat Ho. La. E. WV11: Wed .3C 12
Moat Ho. La. W. WV11: Wed .3C 12
Moat St. WV13: W'hall .2F 19
Mobberley Rd. WV14: Cose .5H 23
Molineux .1D 16 (1A 26)
Molineux All.
WV1: Wolv .1D 16 (1A 26)
(not continuous)
Molineux Fold
WV1: Wolv .1D 16 (1B 26)
Molineux St.
WV1: Wolv .1D 16 (1B 26)
Monmar Ct. WV12: W'hall .5G 13
Monmer Cl. WV13: W'hall .1G 19
Monmer Cl. Ind. Est.
WV13: W'hall .1H 19
Monmer La. WV12: W'hall .6G 13
WV13: W'hall .6G 13
Monmore Bus. Pk. WV2: Wolv .5G 17
MONMORE GREEN .4F 17
Monmore Green Stadium .4H 17
Monmore Pk. Ind. Est.
WV2: E'shll .5G 17
Monmore Rd. WV1: Wolv .4H 17
Monsal Av. WV10: Wolv .6F 11
Monument Dr. WV10: F'stne .1B 6
Monument La. DY3: Sed .5F 23
Moorcroft WV14: Bils .3F 25
Moorcroft Dr. WS10: W'bry .4H 25
Moore Cl. WV6: Pert .6C 8
Moore Rd. WV12: W'hall .2H 13
Moore St. WV1: Wolv .3G 17
Moorfield Rd. WV2: Wolv .5D 16
Moorings, The WV9: Pend .6A 4
Moorland Av. WV10: Oxl .4D 10
Moor Pk. WV6: Pert .5A 8
Moor St. Sth. WV2: Wolv .5D 16
Moreton Av. WV4: E'shll .2F 23
Moreton Cl. DY4: Tip .4G 25
Moreton Rd. WV10: Bush .1E 11
Morgan Cl. WV12: W'hall .6G 13
Morgan Dr. WV14: Cose .6A 24
Morley Gro. WV6: Wolv .6D 10
Morrison Av. WV10: Bush .2E 11
Morville Cft. WV14: Bils .2A 24
Mosedale Dr. WV11: Wed .5E 13
MOSELEY
WV10 .4H 5
WV13 .2B 18
Moseley Ct. WV11: Ess .5E 7
WV13: W'hall .3C 18
Moseley Old Hall .3H 5
Moseley Old Hall La.
WV10: F'stne .3H 5
Moseley Pk. Sports Cen. .4D 18
Moseley Rd. WV10: Bush .3G 5
WV13: W'hall .3C 18
Moseley St. WV10: Wolv .6D 10
Moss Gdns. WV14: Cose .3A 24
Mostyn St. WV1: Wolv .6C 10
Mott Cl. DY4: Tip .6H 25
Mount Cl. WV5: Wom .6D 20
Mount Ct. WV6: Tett .2E 15
Mount Dr. WV5: Wom .6D 20
Mountford La. WV14: Bils .5C 18
Mount Gdns. WV8: Cod .4C 2
Mt. Pleasant WV14: Bils .6D 18
Mt. Pleasant St. WV14: Cose .6A 24
Mount Rd. WV4: E'shll .4G 23
WV4: Penn .1B 22
WV5: Wom .6D 20
WV6: Tett .2D 14
WV13: W'hall .4D 18
Mountwood Covert WV6: Tett .1E 15
Moxhull Cl. WV12: W'hall .1H 13
Moxhull Gdns. WV12: W'hall .1H 13
MOXLEY .2G 25
Moxley Ct. WS10: Mox .2F 25
Moxley Ind. Cen. WS10: Mox .2H 25
Moxley Rd. WS10: Darl .2G 25
Muchall Rd. WV4: Penn .1B 22
Mullett Rd. WV11: Wed .3A 12
Murdoch Rd. WV14: Bils .6F 19
Myatt Av. WV2: E'shll .6F 17
Myatt Cl. WV2: E'shll .6F 17
Myrtle Gro. WV3: Wolv .6H 15
Myrtle St. WV2: E'shll .6G 17
Myrtle Ter. DY4: Tip .4G 25

N

Nailors Fold WV14: Cose .4C 24
Nally Dr. WV14: Cose .4H 23
Napier Rd. WV2: Wolv .5E 17
Naseby Rd. WV6: Pert .1C 14
Nash Av. WV6: Pert .1B 14
Navigation St. WV1: Wolv .3F 17
NEACHELLS .2C 18
Neachells La. WV11: Wed .5C 12
WV13: W'hall .2C 18
Neachells La. Ind. Est.
WV11: Wed .6C 12
Neale Ho. *WV2: Wolv* .*5D 16*
(off Blakenhall Gdns.)
Needwood Cl. WV2: Wolv .6C 16
Needwood Dr. WV4: E'shll .2G 23
Nelson Av. WV14: Bils .5B 18
Nelson St. WV2: Wolv .4D 16 (6B 26)
WV13: W'hall .1G 19
Neptune Ind. Est. WV13: W'hall .4G 19
Netherby Rd. DY3: Sed .6D 22
Nethy Dr. WV6: Tett .5E 9
Neve Av. WV10: Bush .1G 11
Neve's Opening WV1: Wolv .2G 17
Neville Av. WV4: Penn .1E 23
Nevis Cl. WV3: Wolv .2H 15
Nevis Gro. WV12: W'hall .1G 13
Newark Rd. WV12: W'hall .3H 13
NEWBOLDS .4H 11
Newbolds Rd. WV10: Wolv .4H 11
Newbolt Rd. WV14: Bils .6D 18
NEWBRIDGE .1H 15
Newbridge Av. WV6: Wolv .1H 15
Newbridge Cres. WV6: Wolv .6H 9
Newbridge Dr. WV6: Wolv .6H 9
Newbridge Gdns. WV6: Wolv .6H 9
Newbridge M. WV6: Wolv .6A 10
Newbridge St. WV6: Wolv .6A 10
Newbury Rd. WV10: F'hses .6D 4
Newcott Cl. WV9: Pend .6A 4
NEW CROSS .5H 11
New Cross Av. WV10: Wolv .6A 12
WV11: Wed .6A 12
NEW CROSS HOSPITAL
(WOLVERHAMPTON) .5A 12
New Cross Ind. Est. WV1: Wolv .1H 17
Newent Cl. WV12: W'hall .1H 19
New Ent. Cen. WV1: Wolv .4H 17
Newey Rd. WV11: Wed .2F 13
New Hall St. WV13: W'hall .2F 19
Newhall St. DY4: Tip .6D 24
Newhampton Ho.
WV1: Wolv .1C 16 (1A 26)
New Hampton Rd. E.
WV1: Wolv .1C 16 (1A 26)
New Hampton Rd. W.
WV6: Wolv .6A 10
New Heath Cl. WV11: Wed .5A 12
Newlands Cl. WV13: W'hall .3F 19
Newman Av. WV4: E'shll .2G 23
Newman Pl. WV14: Bils .5E 19
Newman Rd. DY4: Tip .5H 25
WV10: Bush .1H 11
Newmarket Cl. WV6: Wolv .5B 10
Newport St. WV10: Wolv .6F 11
New Railway St. WV13: W'hall .2G 19
New Rd. WS10: Darl .6H 19
WV6: Wolv .6H 9
WV10: Bush .2A 12
WV10: C Grn, S Hth .1A 6
WV13: W'hall .3F 19
New St. WS10: Darl .6H 19
WV2: E'shll .6H 17
WV3: Wolv .5G 15
WV4: E'shll .1F 23
WV11: Ess .5F 7
WV13: W'hall .3D 18
Newton Ct. WV9: Pend .5A 4
Newton Ho. WV13: W'hall .3G 19
New Villas WV11: Wed .5H 11
Nicholds Cl. WV14: Cose .5A 24
Nicholls Fold WV11: Wed .5C 12
Nicholls Rd. DY4: Tip .5D 24
Nightingale Cres.
WV12: W'hall .2G 13
Nightingale Pl. WV14: Bils .6C 18
Nine Elms La. WV10: Wolv .5F 11
Nocke Rd. WV11: Wed .1E 13
Noose Cres. WV13: W'hall .2D 18
Noose La. WV13: W'hall .2D 18
Norbury Cres. WV4: E'shll .2G 23
Norbury Rd. WV10: Wolv .4G 11
WV14: Bils .6E 19
Nordley Rd. WV11: Wed .5B 12
Nordley Wlk. WV11: Wed .4B 12
Norfolk Rd. WV3: Wolv .4B 16
Northam Wlk. WV6: Wolv .6C 10
North Av. WV11: Wed .4B 12
Northcott Rd. WV14: Bils .2D 24
North Cres. WV10: F'stne .1A 6
North Dale WV6: Tett .6E 9
Northfield Gro. WV3: Wolv .5F 15
North Grn. WV4: Penn .6G 15
Northicote Recreation &
Community Cen. .5F 5
North One M. DY3: Sed .5D 22
Northover Cl. WV9: Pend .6B 4
North Rd. DY4: Tip .6G 25
WV1: Wolv .6D 10
Nth. Springfield DY3: Sed .5F 23
North St. WV1: Wolv .2D 16 (2B 26)
(not continuous)
Northway DY3: Sed .3D 22
(Alderdale Av.)
DY3: Sed .5C 22
(Sunningdale Rd.)
Northwood Pk. Cl. WV10: Bush .5E 5
Northwood Pk. Rd. WV10: Bush .5F 5
Northycote Farm Country Pk. .5H 5
Northycote La. WV10: Bush .4G 5
Norton Cl. WV4: Penn .3F 21
Norton Cres. WV14: Cose .5C 24
Nottingham Dr. WV12: W'hall .3H 13
Nursery Gdns. WV8: Cod .4C 2
Nursery St. WV1: Wolv .1D 16 (1B 26)
Nursery Wlk. WV6: Tett .6G 9
Nutley Dr. DY4: Tip .6H 25

O

Oak Cl. DY4: Tip .5F 25
OAKEN .6A 2
Oaken Covert WV8: Cod .6B 2
Oaken Dr. WV8: Cod, Oaken .6A 2
Oaken Gro. WV8: Cod .6B 2
Oaken La. WV8: Oaken .5A 2
Oaken Lanes WV8: Cod .5B 2
Oaken Pk. WV8: Cod .6D 2
Oakfield Rd. WV8: Bilb .6E 3
Oak Grn. WV6: Tett .1E 15
Oak Gro. WV11: Wed .3A 12
Oak Hill WV3: Wolv .4F 15
Oaklands, The WV3: Wolv .4C 16
Oaklands Grn. WV14: Bils .4C 18
Oaklands Rd. WV3: Wolv .4C 16
Oakleigh Dr. WV8: Bilb .5D 2
Oakley Cl. WV4: Penn .1G 21
Oakley Gro. WV4: Penn .1G 21
Oakley Rd. WV4: Penn .1G 21
Oak Leys WV3: Wolv .3F 15
Oakridge Cl. WV12: W'hall .6H 13
Oakridge Dr. WV12: W'hall .6H 13
Oak Rd. WV13: W'hall .2D 18
Oaks, The WV3: Wolv .2B 16
Oaks Cres. WV3: Wolv .3B 16
Oaks Dr. WV3: Wolv .2B 16
WV10: B'frd .1G 5
Oak St. WV3: Wolv .3B 16
Oaktree Ri. WV8: Cod .4B 2
Oakwood Cl. WV11: Ess .5G 7
Oatlands Way WV6: Pert .1A 14
OCKER HILL .6H 25
Ocker Hill Rd. DY4: Tip .5G 25
O'Connor Dr. DY4: Tip .5H 25
Offa's Dr. WV6: Pert .5B 8
Okement Dr. WV11: Wed .5A 12
Olde Hall Ct. WV10: F'stne .1B 6
Olde Hall Rd. WV10: F'stne .1B 6
OLD FALLINGS .2G 11
Old Fallings Cres. WV10: Bush .3F 11
Old Fallings La. WV10: Bush .1G 11
Old Farm Dr. WV8: Bilb .4D 2
Old Farm Mdw. WV3: Wolv .4F 15
Oldfield Rd. WV14: Cose .6H 23
Old Hall St. WV1: Wolv .3E 17 (4C 26)
Old Hampton La. WV10: Bush .6A 6
Old Heath Cres. WV1: Wolv .3H 17
Old Heath Rd. WV1: Wolv .3H 17
Old Hill WV6: Tett .5G 9
Old Landywood La. WV11: Ess .2H 7
Old La. WV6: Tett .2C 14
WV10: F'stne .1B 6
Old Mnr., The WV6: Tett .5G 9
Old Meeting Rd. WV14: Cose .6B 24
OLD MOXLEY .2F 25
Old School Cl. WV13: W'hall .2F 19
Old Stow Heath La. WV1: Wolv .3B 18
Old Warstone La. WV11: Ess .1G 7
Olga Dr. DY4: Tip .5G 25
Olinthus Av. WV11: Wed .3D 12
Olive Av. WV4: E'shll .1F 23
Oliver Cres. WV14: Bils .4D 24
Orchard, The WV6: Tett .4H 9
WV14: Bils .1D 24
Orchard Cl. WV3: Wolv .5E 15
WV13: W'hall .3G 19
Orchard Cres. WV3: Wolv .5E 15
Orchard Gro. WV4: Penn .2B 22
Orchard La. WV8: Bilb .5E 3
Orchard Rd. WV11: Wed .3B 12
WV13: W'hall .3G 19
Oriel Dr. WV10: F'hses .5E 5
Ormes La. WV6: Tett .1F 15
Ormond Pl. WV14: Bils .6E 19
Orslow Wlk. WV10: Wolv .5H 11
ORTON .3C 20
Orton Gro. WV4: Penn .2G 21
Orton La. WV4: Lwr P .3C 20
WV5: Wom .3C 20
Orwell Cl. WV11: Wed .5E 13
Osborne Dr. WS10: Darl .4H 19
Osborne Rd. WV4: Penn .1A 22
Osier Pl. WV1: Wolv .2G 17
Osier St. WV1: Wolv .2G 17
Otterstone Cl. DY3: Sed .4D 22
Overdale Cl. WS2: Wals .1H 19
Overdale Dr. WV13: W'hall .1H 19
Overfield Dr. WV14: Cose .3H 23
Overseal Rd. WV11: Wed .2D 12
Overstrand WV9: Pend .5A 4
Overton Wlk. WV4: Penn .6F 15
Owen Pl. WV14: Bils .6C 18
Owen Rd. WV3: Wolv .3B 16
WV13: W'hall .3H 19
WV14: Bils .5C 18
Owen Rd. Ind. Est.
WV13: W'hall .3H 19
Oxbarn Av. WV3: Wolv .6H 15
Oxford St. WV1: Wolv .3F 17 (4D 26)
WV14: Bils .1D 24
Oxford St. Ind. Est. WV14: Bils .1E 25
OXLEY .2C 10
Oxley Av. WV10: Oxl .4D 10
Oxley Ct. Cvn. Pk. WV10: Oxl .2B 10
Oxley La. WV1: Wolv .1D 16
Oxley Links Rd. WV10: Oxl .2C 10
Oxley Moor Rd. WV9: Pend .2B 10
WV10: Oxl .2B 10
Oxley St. WV1: Wolv .6D 10
Oxted Cl. WV11: Wed .5E 13

P

Pace Cres. WV14: Bils .4F 25
Packwood Cl. WV13: W'hall .4E 19
Padarn Cl. DY3: Sed .5D 22
Padbury WV9: Pend .5C 4
Paddock, The WV4: Penn .6C 16
WV6: Pert .6A 8
WV8: Cod .6C 2
WV14: Cose .5C 24
Paddock Vw. WV6: Wolv .4C 10
Paget Cl. WV14: Cose .6A 24
Paget Rd. WV6: Wolv .2A 16
Paget St. WV1: Wolv .1C 16 (1A 26)

A-Z Wolverhampton 35

Pagham Cl.—Regent Rd.

Pagham Cl. WV9: Pend 6A 4
Painters Cft. WV14: Cose 5D 24
Palethorpe Rd. DY4: Tip 6F 25
Palmer Cl. WV11: Wed 1E 13
Palmer's Cl. WV8: Bilb 1F 9
PALMER'S CROSS 2G 9
Palmer's Way WV8: Bilb 1F 9
Paradise La. WV10: B'frd, S Hth . . . 1F 5
Park and Ride
Corser St. 3G 17
Plascom 3H 17
Priestfield 5H 17
Science Park 4D 10
Park Av. WV1: Wolv 1C 16 (1A 26)
WV4: Penn 1D 22
WV13: W'hall 2E 19
Park Cres. WV1: Wolv . . . 2C 16 (2A 26)
PARK DALE 1B 16
Parkdale DY3: Sed 6E 23
Park Dale Ct. WV1: Wolv 1B 16
Park Dale E. WV1: Wolv 1B 16
Park Dale W. WV1: Wolv 1B 16
Park Dr. WV4: Penn 1D 22
Parker Paul Ind. Est.
WV2: Wolv 5D 16
Parker Rd. WV11: Wed 1E 13
Parkes Av. WV8: Cod 6E 3
Parkes La. DY4: Tip 6E 25
Parkes St. WV13: W'hall 3G 19
PARKFIELD 1G 23
Parkfield Chalet Land (Cvn. Pk.)
WV2: Wolv 6E 17
Parkfield Colliery WV4: E'shll . . . 1G 23
Parkfield Cres. WV2: E'shll 6F 17
Parkfield Gro. WV2: E'shll 6F 17
Parkfield Rd. WV4: E'shll 6E 17
Park Hall Rd. WV4: Penn 2E 23
Park Ho. WV11: Ess 5F 7
Parkhouse Av. WV11: Wed 4A 12
Parklands, The WV3: Wolv 3G 15
Parklands Rd. WV1: Wolv 3H 17
WV14: Cose 4C 24
Park La. WV10: Bush, Wolv 4F 11
Park Lane Trad. Est.
WV10: Wolv 5F 11
Park Mdw. Av. WV14: Bils 4B 18
Park Ri. WV3: Wolv 2H 15
Park Rd. WV10: F'stne 1C 6
WV13: W'hall 1E 19
WV14: Bils 1B 24
Park Rd. E. WV1: Wolv 1C 16
Park Rd. W. WV1: Wolv 1B 16
Parks Cres. WV11: Ess 5F 7
Parkside Av. WV13: W'hall 2D 18
Parkside Ind. Est. WV1: Wolv . . . 3G 17
Park St. WS10: Darl 1H 25
Park St. Sth. WV2: Wolv 6D 16
Park Ter. WS10: Darl 6G 19
Park Vw. WS10: Darl 6H 19
Park Vw. Rd. WV14: Bils 4B 18
PARK VILLAGE 5G 11
Park Village Youth Media Activity Cen.
WV10: Wolv 5G 11
Park Way WV11: Wed 1F 13
Parkway, The DY4: Tip 5H 25
WV6: Pert 4A 8
Parkyn St. WV2: Wolv 4F 17
Parry Rd. WV11: Wed 2F 13
Partridge Av. WS10: Darl 6G 19
Pastures, The WV6: Pert 6A 8
Patent Dr. WS10: W'bry 4H 25
Paternoster Row
WV1: Wolv 2D 16 (2A 26)
Patricia Av. WV4: Penn 1D 22
Patrick Gregory Rd.
WV11: Wed 3E 13
Patshull Av. WV10: F'hses 5C 4
Patshull Gro. WV10: F'hses 5C 4
Pattingham Rd. WV6: Pert, Tett . . . 2A 14
Paul Pursehouse Rd.
WV14: Cose 3C 24
Paul St. WV2: Wolv 4D 16 (6A 26)
WV14: Cose 5H 23
Paxton Av. WV6: Pert 1B 14
PDH Ind. Est. WS10: Mox 2H 25
Peach Av. WS10: Darl 6H 19
Peach Rd. WV12: W'hall 4F 13
Peacock Av. WV11: Wed 2F 13
Peacock Rd. WS10: Darl 5G 19
Pearson Ct. WV12: W'hall 6H 13
Pearson St. WV2: Wolv . . 4D 16 (6B 26)
Peartree Av. WV13: W'hall 3G 19
Pear Tree La. WV11: Wed 1A 12
Peartree La. WV14: Cose 6C 24
Peascroft La. WV14: Bils 6D 18
(not continuous)
Peel Cl. WS10: Darl 4H 19
WV13: W'hall 3F 19
Peel St. WV3: Wolv 3D 16 (4A 26)
WV13: W'hall 3F 19
Pelham St. WV3: Wolv 3B 16
Pemberton Rd. WV14: Cose 5C 24
Pembroke Av. WV2: E'shll 5H 17
Pembroke Cl. WV12: W'hall 4H 13
Pencombe Dr. WV4: Penn 1E 23
Penda Gro. WV6: Pert 5C 8
PENDEFORD 5B 4
Pendeford Av. WV6: Tett 2H 9
Pendeford Bus. Pk.
WV9: Pend 5A 4
Pendeford Cl. WV6: Tett 2H 9
Pendeford Hall La.
WV9: Coven, Pend 3E 3
Pendeford Hall Mobile Home Pk.
WV9: Pend 4H 3
Pendeford La. WV9: Pend 4B 4
Pendeford Mill La.
WV8: Bilb 5E 3
Pendene Ct. WV4: Penn 1B 22
Penderell Cl. WV10: F'stne 2H 5
Pendinas Dr. WV8: Bilb 5E 3
Pendrell Cl. WV8: Cod 5D 2
Pendrell Ct. WV8: Cod 5D 2
Pendrill Rd. WV10: Bush 5F 5
Penhallow Dr. WV4: E'shll 1F 23
Penk Ri. WV6: Tett 6D 8
Penleigh Gdns. WV5: Wom 6C 20
PENN 1H 21
Penn Comn. Rd. WV4: Penn 5H 21
Penncroft La. WV4: Penn 5A 22
PENN FIELDS 6B 16
PENN HOSPITAL 2H 21
Pennhouse Av. WV4: Penn 1A 22
Pennine Way WV12: W'hall 5H 13
Penn Rd. DY3: Sed 5A 22
WV2: Wolv 6B 16 (6A 26)
WV3: Wolv 6B 16
WV4: Penn 3G 21
Penn Rd. Island
WV2: Wolv 3D 16 (5A 26)
Penn Rd. Retail Pk.
WV2: Wolv 4D 16
Penn St. WV3: Wolv 4C 16 (6A 26)
Penns Wood Cl. DY3: Sed 4D 22
Pennwood Ct. WV4: Penn 6G 15
Pennwood La. WV4: Penn 3A 22
Pennycress Gdns. WV10: F'stne . . . 1B 6
Penshaw Cl. WV9: Pend 5B 4
Penstone La. WV4: Lwr P 2B 20
Pentland Gdns. WV3: Wolv 2H 15
Penwood Gdns. WV14: Cose 6B 24
Perch Cl. WV10: Wolv 6A 12
Perivale Gro. WV14: Cose 6C 24
Perks Rd. WV11: Wed 1F 13
Perry Av. WV10: Bush 2G 11
Perry Hall Dr. WV12: W'hall 5G 13
Perry Hall Rd. WV11: Wed 4E 13
Perry St. WV14: Bils 3D 24
Perry Trad. Est. WV14: Bils 3D 24
Perth Rd. WV12: W'hall 4G 13
PERTON 6B 8
Perton Brook Va. WV6: Tett 2C 14
Perton Gro. WV6: Tett 2C 14
Perton Rd. WV6: Tett 2B 14
Peter Av. WV14: Bils 4E 25
Peterdale Dr. WV4: Penn 3A 22
Petworth Cl. WV13: W'hall 4E 19
Peverill Rd. WV4: E'shll 3F 23
WV6: Pert 6C 8
Philip St. WV14: Cose 5C 24
Phillips Av. WV11: Wed 1E 13
Phoenix Ind. Est. WV14: Bils 2E 25
Phoenix Ri. *WV2: Wolv 6D 16*
(off Blakenhall Gdns.)
Phoenix Rd. WV11: Wed 1C 18
Phoenix Rd. Ind. Est.
WV11: Wed 1C 18
Phoenix St. WV2: Wolv 6E 17
Pickering Rd. WV11: Wed 5C 12
Pickrell Rd. WV14: Cose 5A 24
Pickwick Pl. WV14: Bils 2D 24
Pimbury Rd. WV12: W'hall 4H 13
Pine Cl. WV3: Wolv 3B 16
Pines, The WV3: Wolv 3G 15
Pine Wlk. WV8: Cod 6C 2
Pineways Dr. WV6: Wolv 6H 9
Pinewood Cl. WV3: Wolv 4D 14
Pinfold Ct. WS10: Darl 1H 25
Pinfold Cres. WV4: Penn 6G 15
Pinfold Gdns. WV11: Wed 5C 12
Pinfold Gro. WV4: Penn 6G 15
Pinfold La. WV4: Penn 6G 15
Pinfold St. WS10: Darl 1H 25
(not continuous)
WV14: Bils 1C 24
Pinfold St. Extension
WS10: Darl 1H 25
Pinson Gdns. WV13: W'hall 2E 19
Pinson Rd. WV13: W'hall 2E 19
Piper Cl. WV6: Pert 6C 8
Piper Rd. WV3: Wolv 4F 15
Piper's Row
WV1: Wolv 2E 17 (3D 26)
Pipes Mdw. WV14: Bils 1D 24
Pirbright Cl. WV14: Bils 3D 24
Pirrey Cl. WV14: Cose 5D 24
Pitt St. WV3: Wolv 3D 16 (4A 26)
Planetary Ind. Est.
WV13: W'hall 1B 18
Planetary Rd. WV13: W'hall 6A 12
Plascom Rd. WV1: Wolv 3H 17
Ploughmans Wlk.
WV8: Pend 1H 9
Plover Cl. WV10: F'stne 1A 6
Plym Cl. WV11: Wed 5B 12
Pointon Cl. WV14: Cose 4H 23
Pond La. WV2: Wolv 4E 17
Poole Cres. WV14: Cose 4C 24
Pool Hall Cres. WV3: Wolv 4C 14
Pool Hall Rd. WV3: Wolv 4C 14
Pool Hayes La. WV12: W'hall 5F 13
Pool Rd. WV11: Wed 4F 13
Pool St. WV2: Wolv 4D 16 (6A 26)
(not continuous)
Pope Rd. WV10: Bush 2H 11
Popes La. WV6: Tett 4D 8
Poplar Av. WV11: Wed 3A 12
Poplar Rd. WV3: Wolv 6B 16
WV14: Bils 5E 19
Poplars Dr. WV8: Cod 6C 2
Poplar St. WV2: Wolv 6E 17
Portchester Dr. WV11: Wed 5C 12
Porthouse Gro. WV14: Cose 3A 24
Portland Pl. WV14: Cose 6A 24
Port La. WV9: Coven 2E 3
PORTOBELLO 4D 18
Portobello Cl. WV13: W'hall 3C 18
Portrush Rd. WV6: Pert 6A 8
Portsdown Cl. WV10: Bush 3G 11
Portswood Cl. WV9: Pend 1A 10
Portway Rd. WV14: Bils 5D 18
Pountney St.
WV2: Wolv 4D 16 (6A 26)
Powell Pl. WV14: Bils 3D 24
Powell St. WV10: Wolv 6G 11
Powis Av. DY4: Tip 6H 25
Powlett St. WV2: Wolv . . . 3E 17 (5D 26)
Poynings, The WV6: Tett 5F 9
Precinct, The WV12: W'hall 5G 13
Prestons Row WV14: Cose 3H 23
Prestwood Av. WV11: Wed 3C 12
Prestwood Rd. WV11: Wed 5H 11
Prestwood Rd. W.
WV11: Wed 4H 11
Price Cres. WV14: Bils 5C 18
Price St. WV14: Bils 1E 25
PRIESTFIELD 6A 18
Priestfield WV2: E'shll 5H 17
Priestfield St. WV14: Bils 6A 18
Primrose Av. DY4: Tip 6H 25
WV10: F'hses, Bush 5E 5
Primrose Gdns. WV8: Cod 5D 2
WV10: F'stne 1A 6
Primrose La. WV10: Bush 4F 5
(Cromwell Rd.)
WV10: Bush 2G 11
(Old Fallings La.)
Prince Charles Rd. WV14: Bils . . . 3E 25
Princes Dr. WV8: Cod 5D 2
PRINCES END 6E 25
Princes End Ind. Est.
DY4: Tip 5D 24
Princes Gdns. WV8: Cod 5C 2
Princess All.
WV1: Wolv 2E 17 (3C 26)
Princess Anne Rd.
WV14: Bils 3E 25
Princess Ct. WV10: Wolv 4H 11
Princes Sq. WV1: Wolv . . . 2E 17 (2C 26)
Princess Sq. WV14: Bils 3E 25
Princess St.
WV1: Wolv 2E 17 (3C 26)
Princess Way WS10: Darl 4H 19
Princeton Gdns. WV9: Pend 6A 4
Priory, The DY3: Sed 6E 23
Priory Ct. WV1: Wolv 1D 16 (1A 26)
Priory Fld. Cl. WV14: Cose 5G 23
Priory La. DY3: Sed 6E 23
Pritchard Av. WV11: Wed 4D 12
Pritchett Av. WV4: E'shll 3G 23
Probert Rd. WV10: Oxl 2B 10
Prole St. WV10: Wolv 6F 11
Prospect St. DY4: Tip 5H 25
WV14: Bils 6D 18
Prosser St. WV10: Wolv 5F 11
WV14: Bils 1C 24
Prouds La. WV14: Bils 4C 18
Provence Cl. WV10: Wolv 6G 11
Providence Row WV14: Cose 6A 24
Pruden Av. WV4: E'shll 3G 23
Pugh Rd. WV14: Bils 3D 24
WV14: Cose 4G 23
Pugin Cl. WV6: Pert 1A 14
Pump St. WV2: E'shll 5H 17
Purbrook Rd. WV1: Wolv 4G 17
Purcel Rd. WV10: Bush 2E 11
Purdy Rd. WV14: Bils 4D 24
Purslet Rd. WV1: Wolv 3H 17

Q

Quadrant, The DY3: Sed 5E 23
Quadrille Lawns WV9: Pend 6A 4
Quail Grn. WV6: Tett 2C 14
Qualcast Rd. WV1: Wolv 2G 17
Quatford Gdns. WV10: Wolv 5F 11
Queen's Arc.
WV1: Wolv 2D 16 (3B 26)
Queens Ct. WV10: Wolv 4H 11
Queens Cres. WV14: Cose 5H 23
Queens Gdns. WV8: Cod 5C 2
WV14: Bils 5C 18
Queens Lea WV12: W'hall 5H 13
Queen Sq. WV1: Wolv 2D 16 (3B 26)
Queens Rd. DY3: Sed 6F 23
Queen St. DY4: Tip 6E 25
WS10: Darl 4H 19
WV1: Wolv 2E 17 (3C 26)
(not continuous)
WV14: Bils 1D 24
(Bridge St.)
WV14: Bils 2G 25
(Tudor Rd.)
Quilter Cl. WV14: Cose 6H 23

R

Rabbit La. WV10: F'stne 1H 5
Raby St. WV2: Wolv 4E 17 (6D 26)
Racecourse Rd. WV6: Wolv 5B 10
Racecourse Rd. Ind. Est.
WV6: Wolv 5B 10
Rachel Cl. DY4: Tip 5H 25
Radford La. WV3: Wolv 6C 14
WV4: Lwr P 6C 14
Radnor Rd. DY3: Sed 6D 22
Radstock Rd. WV12: W'hall 1H 13
Raglan Av. WV6: Pert 1C 14
Raglan St. WV3: Wolv . . . 2C 16 (3A 26)
Ragley Dr. WV13: W'hall 4E 19
Railway Dr. WV1: Wolv . . . 2E 17 (2D 26)
WV14: Bils 1D 24
Railway La. WV13: W'hall 3F 19
Railway St. WV1: Wolv . . . 2E 17 (2D 26)
WV13: W'hall 3F 19
WV14: Bils 1D 24
Rainbow St. WV2: Wolv 4D 16
WV14: Cose 3C 24
Raleigh Rd. WV14: Bils 3E 25
Randall Lines Ho. WV1: Wolv 1D 16
Ranelagh Ho. *WV2: Wolv 5E 17*
(off Blakenhall Gdns.)
Ranelagh Rd. WV2: Wolv 6D 16
Ranworth Ri. WV4: Penn 2E 23
Ratcliffe Rd. WV11: Wed 4F 13
Rathbone Cl. WV14: Bils 1C 24
Rathlin Cl. WV9: Pend 5B 4
Rathwell Cl. WV9: Pend 6B 4
Raven Cres. WV11: Wed 2E 13
Ravenhill Dr. WV8: Cod 5D 2
Ravensbourne Gro.
WV13: W'hall 2H 19
Ravenscroft Rd.
WV12: W'hall 5G 13
Ravensholme WV6: Tett 2C 14
Rayleigh Rd. WV3: Wolv 4B 16
Raymond Gdns. WV11: Wed 5D 12
Raynor Rd. WV10: Wolv 4G 11
Reansway Sq. WV6: Wolv 6B 10
Reapers Wlk. WV8: Pend 1A 10
Rebecca Gdns. WV4: Penn 2A 22
Redacres WV6: Tett 4H 9
Redcar Rd. WV10: F'hses 4E 5
Redcott's Cl. WV10: Bush 2H 11
Red Cross Wlk. WV1: Wolv 1D 16
Red Hill St. WV1: Wolv 1D 16
Redhouse Rd. WV6: Tett 5D 8
Redhurst Dr. WV10: F'hses 5C 4
Red La. DY3: Sed 6C 22
WV11: Ess 1H 13
Red Lion St.
WV1: Wolv 2D 16 (2A 26)
Redmoor Gdns. WV4: Penn 1B 22
Redoak Ho. WV10: Wolv 1G 17
Red Rock Dr. WV8: Cod 6C 2
Redstone Dr. WV11: Wed 5E 13
Redwood Rd. WV14: Cose 4C 24
Redwood Way WV12: W'hall 2G 13
Reedham Gdns. WV4: Penn 1G 21
Reedly Rd. WV12: W'hall 1H 13
Reeves Gdns. WV8: Cod 4D 2
Reflex Ind. Pk. WV13: W'hall 1E 19
Regency Ct.
WV1: Wolv 1D 16 (1A 26)
Regent Ho. WV1: Wolv . . . 1C 16 (2A 26)
Regent Rd. WV4: Penn 1H 21

Snow Hill Junc.—Tyning Cl.

Snow Hill Junc.
WV2: Wolv ... 3E 17 (5C 26)
Soberton Cl. WV11: Wed ... 3E 13
Solari Cl. DY4: Tip ... 6H 25
Solent Cl. WV9: Pend ... 6A 4
Solva Cl. WV1: Wolv ... 3A 18
Somerford Gdns. WV10: Bush ... 6F 5
Somerford Pl. WV13: W'hall ... 3E 19
Somerford Way WV14: Cose ... 6A 24
Sonning Dr. WV9: Pend ... 6A 4
Sorrel Cl. WV10: F'stne ... 1A 6
Southall Cres. WV14: Cose ... 5B 24
Southall Rd. WV11: Wed ... 2F 13
Southampton St.
WV1: Wolv ... 1E 17 (1D 26)
South Av. WV11: Wed ... 5B 12
Southbourne Rd. WV10: F'hses ... 5D 4
South Cres. WV10: F'stne ... 2A 6
Southerndown Rd. DY3: Sed ... 6C 22
Southern Way WS10: Mox ... 3H 25
WS10: W'bry ... 3H 25
Southfield Gro. WV3: Wolv ... 5F 15
Southfield Rd. WV11: Wed ... 5E 13
Southgate WV1: Wolv ... 2C 16
South Grn. WV4: Penn ... 1G 21
South Rd. DY4: Tip ... 6G 25
South Staffordshire Golf Course ... 4G 9
South St. WV10: Oxl ... 4D 10
WV13: W'hall ... 3E 19
South View Cl. WV8: Bilb ... 6E 3
WV10: F'stne ... 2A 6
South Vw. Rd. DY3: Sed ... 6D 22
Southwick Pl. WV14: Bils ... 5C 18
Speedwell Cl. WV11: Wed ... 5D 12
Speedwell Gdns. WV10: F'stne ... 1A 6
Spencer Av. WV14: Cose ... 6B 24
Spenser Av. WV6: Pert ... 6C 8
Spinney, The WV3: Wolv ... 3G 15
Spiral Ct. WV11: Wed ... 3C 12
Spondon Rd. WV11: Wed ... 2D 12
SPRING BANK ... 1G 19
Spring Bank Ho. WV13: W'hall ... 1F 19
Spring Dr. Ind. Est. WV4: E'shll ... 2H 23
SPRINGFIELD ... 1F 17
Springfield Av. DY3: Sed ... 5F 23
Springfield Grn. DY3: Sed ... 5F 23
Springfield Gro. DY3: Sed ... 5E 23
Springfield La. WV10: F'hses ... 4E 5
Springfield Rd. WV10: Wolv ... 6F 11
WV14: Bils ... 5D 18
SPRING HILL ... 2F 21
SPRINGHILL
Essington ... 3H 7
Springhill Av. WV4: Penn ... 3F 21
Springhill Cl. WV12: W'hall ... 3H 13
Springhill Gro. WV4: Penn ... 2F 21
Springhill La. WV4: Lwr P ... 1C 20
WV4: Penn ... 3F 21
Springhill Pk. WV4: Penn ... 3E 21
Springhill Rd. WV11: Wed ... 2D 12
Spring Hill Ter. WV4: Penn ... 6B 16
Spring La. WV12: W'hall ... 6G 13
Spring Mdws. Cl. WV8: Bilb ... 4E 3
Spring Rd. WV4: E'shll ... 1H 23
Spring Rd. Ind. Est.
WV4: E'shll ... 2H 23
Spring St. DY4: Tip ... 6H 25
SPRING VALE ... 2A 24
Springvale Av. WV14: Bils ... 2A 24
Springvale Bus. Cen.
WV14: Bils ... 2A 24
Spring Va. Cl. WV14: Cose ... 5H 23
Spring Va. Ind. Pk. WV14: Bils ... 1B 24
Springvale St. WV13: W'hall ... 1G 19
Springvale Way WV14: Bils ... 2B 24
Sproat Av. WS10: Darl ... 1H 25
Spruce Way WV3: Wolv ... 3G 15
Spur Tree Av. WV3: Wolv ... 3D 14
Square, The WV2: Wolv ... 4E 17
WV8: Cod ... 4C 2
WV12: W'hall ... 2H 13
Squirrel Wlk. WV4: Penn ... 2B 22
Staddlestones, The WV6: Pert ... 6A 8
Stadium Cl. WV13: W'hall ... 1G 19
Stafford Ct. WV10: F'hses ... 3D 4
Stafford La. WV8: Cod ... 1A 8
Stafford Rd. WS10: Darl ... 6H 19
WV10: Cov H ... 1D 4
WV10: F'hses, Oxl, Wolv ... 2D 10
Stafford St. WV1: Wolv ... 6D 10 (1C 26)
WV13: W'hall ... 2F 19
(not continuous)
WV14: Bils ... 1C 24
Stafford St. Junc.
WV1: Wolv ... 1D 16 (1B 26)
Stag Ind. Est. WV14: Bils ... 2E 25
Stanbury Av. WS10: Darl ... 6G 19
Stanford Rd. WV2: Wolv ... 5D 16
Stanhope St.
WV3: Wolv ... 3C 16 (4A 26)
Stanley Cl. WV11: Wed ... 2E 13
Stanley Ct. WV6: Pert ... 6B 8
Stanley Pl. WV14: Bils ... 1A 24
Stanley Rd. WS10: Darl ... 1H 25
WV10: Bush ... 1E 11
Stanton Rd. WV1: Wolv ... 2G 17
Star St. WV3: Wolv ... 4H 15
Station Cl. WV8: Cod ... 5C 2
Station Rd. WV5: Wom ... 6D 20
WV8: Cod ... 5B 2
WV14: Bils ... 1D 24
Station Ter. WV14: Cose ... 5B 24
Staveley Rd. WV1: Wolv ... 6D 10
Stead Cl. DY4: Tip ... 5G 25
Steadman Cft. DY4: Tip ... 6H 25
Steel Dr. WV10: Bush ... 2E 11
Steelhouse La. WV2: Wolv ... 3F 17
Steelpark Way WV11: Wed ... 6C 12
Stenbury Cl. WV10: Bush ... 4G 5
Stephens Cl. WV11: Wed ... 2E 13
Stephenson Dr. WV6: Pert ... 4B 8
Stephenson St. WV3: Wolv ... 3C 16
Steven Dr. WV14: Bils ... 5D 24
Stevens Ga.
WV2: Wolv ... 4D 16 (6B 26)
Stewart St. WV2: Wolv ... 4D 16 (6B 26)
Stirling Cres. WV12: W'hall ... 4G 13
Stirling Rd. WV14: Bils ... 3E 25
Stockbridge Cl. WV6: Tett ... 2C 14
Stockton Ct. WV14: Cose ... 6A 24
STOCKWELL END ... 5G 9
Stockwell End WV6: Tett ... 4G 9
Stockwell Rd. WV6: Tett ... 5G 9
Stokes Av. DY4: Tip ... 6F 25
WV13: W'hall ... 4E 19
Stokesay Av. WV6: Pert ... 1C 14
Stom Rd. WV14: Bils ... 1A 24
Stoneacre Cl. WV3: Wolv ... 3D 14
Stonedown Cl. WV14: Cose ... 3H 23
Stonefield Rd. WV14: Bils ... 1C 24
Stonefield Wlk. *WV14: Bils ... 1C 24*
(off Stonefield Rd.)
Stonehouse Av. WV13: W'hall ... 6E 13
Stoneleigh Gdns. WV8: Cod ... 4C 2
Stone St. WV14: Bils ... 1D 24
Stoney La. WV4: Penn ... 1C 22
Stourbridge Rd. WV4: Penn ... 6F 21
WV5: Wom ... 6F 21
Stourmore Cl. WV12: W'hall ... 4H 13
Stourton Dr. WV4: Penn ... 1F 21
STOW HEATH ... 5A 18
Stowheath La. WV1: Wolv ... 5A 18
Stow Heath Pl. WV1: Wolv ... 5A 18
STOW LAWN ... 4B 18
Stowmans Cl. WV14: Cose ... 3A 24
Straight Rd. WV12: W'hall ... 4H 13
Strathern Dr. WV14: Cose ... 5H 23
Strathfield Wlk. WV4: Penn ... 6F 15
Strathmore Cres. WV5: Wom ... 5D 20
Strathmore Rd. DY4: Tip ... 6F 25
Stratton St. WV10: Wolv ... 6F 11
Strawberry La. WV13: W'hall ... 1B 18
Strawberry La. Ind. Est.
WV13: W'hall ... 2B 18
Strawmoor La. WV8: Oaken, Cod ... 5A 2
Stretton Gdns. WV8: Cod ... 4C 2
Stretton Pl. WV14: Cose ... 5H 23
Stretton Rd. WV12: W'hall ... 2H 13
Stringes Cl. WV13: W'hall ... 1H 19
Stringes La. WV13: W'hall ... 2G 19
Strode Rd. WV2: Wolv ... 6D 16
Stroud Av. WV12: W'hall ... 6H 13
Stroud Cl. WV12: W'hall ... 6H 13
Stubbington Cl. WV13: W'hall ... 3C 18
Stubbs Rd. WV3: Wolv ... 5B 16
Stubby La. WV11: Wed ... 4E 13
Stubley Dr. WV10: Wolv ... 4F 11
Studley Rd. WV3: Wolv ... 4F 15
Suckling Grn. La. WV8: Cod ... 6C 2
Sudbury Cl. WV11: Wed ... 2D 12
Suffolk Cl. WV11: Wed ... 3B 12
SUMMER HILL ... 6F 25
Summer Hill Rd. WV14: Cose ... 5C 24
Summerhill Rd. DY4: Tip ... 6E 25
Summerhouse Rd.
WV14: Cose ... 5H 23
Summer Row
WV2: Wolv ... 3D 16 (4B 26)
Summer St. WV13: W'hall ... 2E 19
Sunbeam St. WV2: Wolv ... 5D 16
Sunbury Cl. WV14: Cose ... 5D 24
Sundour Cres. WV11: Wed ... 1A 12
Sundridge Wlk. WV4: Penn ... 6F 15
Sunningdale Av. WV6: Pert ... 5A 8
Sunningdale Rd. DY3: Sed ... 6C 22
Sunset Pl. WV4: E'shll ... 3G 23
Sun St. WV1: Wolv ... 2F 17
WV10: Wolv ... 2F 17
Surrey Dr. WV3: Wolv ... 3H 15
Sussex Dr. WV3: Wolv ... 3H 15
Sutherland Av. WV2: Wolv ... 4G 17
Sutherland Dr. WV5: Wom ... 6D 20
Sutherland Gro. WV6: Pert ... 6C 8
Sutherland Ho. WV1: Wolv ... 2B 16
Sutherland Pl.
WV2: Wolv ... 3E 17 (5D 26)
Sutherland Rd. WV4: Penn ... 1C 22
Sutton Ct. WV4: E'shll ... 4F 23
Sutton Rd. WS10: Mox ... 1F 25
Swale Gro. WV13: W'hall ... 2H 19
Swallow Ct. WV10: Bush ... 3E 11
Swallowdale WV6: Tett ... 2C 14
Swallowfields Rd. DY3: Sed ... 4D 22
Swan Bank WV4: Penn ... 2A 22
Swancote Dr. WV4: Penn ... 6F 15
Swancroft Rd. DY4: Tip ... 6E 25
Swanmore Cl. WV3: Wolv ... 4H 15
Swann Rd. WV14: Cose ... 4H 23
Swann Wlk. DY4: Tip ... 6F 25
Swan St. WV1: Wolv ... 2G 17
Sweetbriar La. WV12: W'hall ... 5H 13
Sweetbriar Rd. WV2: E'shll ... 5H 17
Sweetman Pl. WV6: Wolv ... 1B 16
Sweetman St. WV6: Wolv ... 6A 10
(not continuous)
Swinford Rd. WV10: Wolv ... 5F 11
Swynnerton Dr. WV11: Ess ... 4E 7
Sycamore Dr. WV3: Wolv ... 3G 15
Sycamore Pl. WV14: Bils ... 3F 25
Sycamores, The WV10: Bush ... 2G 11
Sydenham Rd. WV1: Wolv ... 2A 18

T

Tadmore Cl. WV14: Bils ... 1B 24
Tadworth Cl. WV1: Wolv ... 2H 17
Talaton Cl. WV9: Pend ... 6B 4
Talbot Pl. WV14: Bils ... 6B 18
Talbot Rd. WV2: Wolv ... 6D 16
Tall Trees Cl. WV12: W'hall ... 4H 13
Tamar Gro. WV6: Pert ... 6B 8
WV13: W'hall ... 2H 19
Tame St. WV14: Bils ... 1E 25
Tanfield Cl. WV6: Tett ... 1E 15
Tanglewood Gro. DY3: Sed ... 4D 22
Tangmere Cl. WV6: Pert ... 5B 8
Tansley Vw. WV2: Wolv ... 5E 17
Tarmac Rd. WV4: E'shll ... 1A 24
Tasman Gro. WV6: Pert ... 5B 8
Taunton Av. WV10: F'hses ... 4E 5
Taverners Cl. WV12: W'hall ... 1H 13
Taylor Rd. WV4: E'shll ... 1G 23
Taylor St. WV11: Wed ... 5C 12
Teal Gro. WS10: Mox ... 3G 25
Teasel Gro. WV10: F'stne ... 1A 6
Teasel Rd. WV11: Wed ... 5D 12
Tebworth Cl. WV9: Pend ... 6A 4
Teesdale Cl. WV1: Wolv ... 2H 17
Telford Gdns. WV3: Wolv ... 5G 15
Teme Gro. WV13: W'hall ... 2H 19
Tempest St. WV2: Wolv ... 3E 17 (4C 26)
Templars Wlk. WV13: W'hall ... 1F 19
Temple Bar WV13: W'hall ... 2F 19
Temple Rd. WV13: W'hall ... 1F 19
Temple Sq. WV13: W'hall ... 1G 19
Temple St.
WV2: Wolv ... 3D 16 (4B 26)
WV14: Bils ... 1D 24
Tenbury Cl. WS2: Wals ... 1H 19
Tenbury Ct. WV4: Penn ... 1G 21
Tenbury Gdns. WV4: Penn ... 2G 21
Tennyson Rd. WV10: Bush ... 1H 11
Tern Cl. WV4: E'shll ... 3E 23
Terrace, The WV3: Wolv ... 3F 15
TETTENHALL ... 6F 9
Tettenhall Rd. WV6: Wolv ... 6H 9
TETTENHALL WOOD ... 2D 14
Teviot Gdns. WV8: Bilb ... 3D 2
Thames Gdns. WV14: Cose ... 5H 23
Thetford Gdns. WV11: Wed ... 4C 12
Third Av. WV10: Bush ... 3F 11
Thirlmere Cl. WV6: Tett ... 2G 9
Thirlmere Dr. WV11: Ess ... 6F 7
Thirlmere Gro. WV6: Pert ... 6C 8
Thirlmere Rd. WV6: Tett ... 2G 9
Thirston Cl. WV11: Wed ... 5F 13
Thistle Cft. WV11: Wed ... 5C 12
Thistledown Dr. WV10: F'stne ... 1H 5
Thistledown Wlk. DY3: Sed ... 5D 22
Thomas Mason Cl. WV11: Wed ... 3C 12
Thomas St. WV2: Wolv ... 4D 16 (6B 26)
Thompson Av. WV2: Wolv ... 5E 17
Thompson Cl. WV13: W'hall ... 1F 19
Thompson Ho. DY4: Tip ... 6H 25
Thompson St. WV13: W'hall ... 1F 19
WV14: Bils ... 1C 24
Thornbury Ct. WV6: Pert ... 1D 14
Thorne Av. WV10: Bush ... 3F 11
Thorne Rd. WV13: W'hall ... 1F 19
Thorne St. WV2: E'shll ... 5H 17
Thorneycroft La. WV10: Wolv ... 5H 11
Thorneycroft Pl. WV14: Bils ... 3G 25
Thorneycroft Rd. WV14: Bils ... 3F 25
Thornley Cl. WV11: Wed ... 1E 13
Thornley Rd. WV11: Wed ... 1E 13
Thornley St.
WV1: Wolv ... 2E 17 (2C 26)
Thornton Rd. WV1: Wolv ... 3A 18
Three Tuns La. WV10: Oxl ... 6D 4
Three Tuns Pde.
WV10: Oxl ... 6D 4
Thrushel Wlk. WV11: Wed ... 5B 12
Thurlstone Dr. WV4: Penn ... 2A 22
Tibberton Cl. WV3: Wolv ... 5G 15
Tibbington Rd. DY4: Tip ... 6D 24
Tibbington Ter. DY4: Tip ... 6D 24
Tiffany La. WV9: Pend ... 6A 4
Tilbury Cl. WV3: Wolv ... 4D 14
Tildesley Dr. WV12: W'hall ... 5G 13
Timmis Cl. WV14: Cose ... 3A 24
Tinacre Hill WV6: Tett ... 2B 14
Tintagel Cl. WV6: Pert ... 1C 14
Tintern Ct. WV6: Pert ... 6B 8
Tipton Ind. Est.
WV14: Cose ... 6C 24
Tipton Leisure Cen. ... 5F 25
Tipton Rd. DY3: Sed ... 6F 23
Tipton St. DY3: Sed ... 6F 23
Tipton Trad. Est.
WV14: Cose ... 6C 24
Titchfield Cl. WV10: Bush ... 4F 5
Tithe Cft. WV10: Wolv ... 1G 17
Tithe Rd. WV11: Wed ... 4C 12
Tobruk Wlk. WV13: W'hall ... 3D 18
Toll End Rd. DY4: Tip ... 6H 25
Tollhouse Way WV5: Wom ... 6B 20
Tolworth Gdns. WV2: Wolv ... 5F 17
Tonadine Cl. WV11: Wed ... 1F 13
Tong Ct. WV1: Wolv ... 6D 10
Torfield WV8: Pend ... 6H 3
Tor Lodge Dr. WV6: Tett ... 2E 15
Torridge Dr. WV11: Wed ... 5B 12
Torridon Rd. WV12: W'hall ... 1G 13
Tor Va. Rd. WV6: Tett ... 2D 14
Tourist Info. Cen.
Wolverhampton ... 2D 16 (3B 26)
Tower St. DY3: Sed ... 5E 23
WV1: Wolv ... 2E 17 (3C 26)
Tower Works Ind. Est.
WV3: Wolv ... 3B 16
Townsend Av. DY3: Sed ... 6E 23
Townson Rd. WV11: Wed ... 2F 13
Townwell Fold
WV1: Wolv ... 2D 16 (3A 26)
Town Yd. WV13: W'hall ... 3F 19
Tozer St. DY4: Tip ... 6E 25
Tractor Spares Ind. Est.
WV13: W'hall ... 2C 18
Tramway Cl. WV14: Bils ... 5E 19
Tranwell Cl. WV9: Pend ... 6A 4
Tree Tops WV5: Wom ... 6B 20
Tremaine Gdns.
WV10: Wolv ... 6E 11
Trent Cl. WV6: Pert ... 6B 8
Trentham Av. WV12: W'hall ... 5F 13
Trentham Ri. WV2: E'shll ... 5G 17
Treynham Cl. WV1: Wolv ... 3B 18
Trident Dr. WS10: W'bry ... 3H 25
Trimpley Gdns.
WV4: Penn ... 3H 21
Tring Ct. WV6: Wolv ... 6A 10
Trinity Ct. WV3: Wolv ... 2B 16
WV13: W'hall ... 3D 18
Trinity Rd. WV12: W'hall ... 4H 13
WV14: Bils ... 1E 25
(not continuous)
Troon Ct. WV6: Pert ... 5A 8
Tryon Pl. WV14: Bils ... 6D 18
TRYSULL ... 5A 20
Trysull Gdns. WV3: Wolv ... 5G 15
Trysull Rd. WV3: Wolv ... 5G 15
WV5: Wom ... 6B 20
Tudor Ct. WV11: Ess ... 5E 7
Tudor Cres. WV2: Wolv ... 6C 16
Tudor Rd. WV10: Wolv ... 6H 11
WV14: Bils ... 2G 25
Tunnel St. WV14: Cose ... 6B 24
Turls Hill Rd. DY3: Sed ... 6F 23
WV14: Cose ... 6F 23
Turls St. DY3: Sed ... 6F 23
Turnberry Cl. WV6: Pert ... 5A 8
Turner Av. WV14: Cose ... 4G 23
Turner Gro. WV6: Pert ... 6D 8
Turner St. DY4: Tip ... 6E 25
Turnham Grn. WV6: Pert ... 1B 14
Turnstone Dr.
WV10: F'stne ... 1A 6
Turton Rd. DY4: Tip ... 5E 25
Turtons Cft. WV14: Cose ... 3A 24
Tutbury Av. WV6: Pert ... 1C 14
Tuxford Cl. WV10: Wolv ... 6F 11
Twyford Gro. WV11: Wed ... 3E 13
Tyburn Rd. WV1: Wolv ... 3B 18
Tyler Gdns. WV13: W'hall ... 3G 19
Tyler Rd. WV13: W'hall ... 4F 19
Tynedale Cres. WV4: E'shll ... 3F 23
Tyning Cl. WV9: Pend ... 6B 4

38 A-Z Wolverhampton

The representation on the maps of a road, track or footpath is no evidence of the existence of a right of way.

The Grid on this map is the National Grid taken from Ordnance Survey mapping with the permission of the Controller of Her Majesty's Stationery Office.